'Carter writes as if he has ADD, careering through his life on oil rigs in exotic locations. He won't win the Booker, but his yarns burn with anarchic energy . . . in a word, irrepressible.'

Herald Sun

'This is one of the most split-my-sides-laughing memoirs I think I have ever read . . . that blows along like the North Sea.'

Northern Star

'Not so much a thriller as a driller, *Don't Tell Mum* is our tip for Bloke's Book of the Year (BBOTY).'

Sunday Telegraph

'What you have here . . . is that rare situation of somebody who not only has a story to tell but the ability to tell it. Carter's anecdotes are told with great good humour and perfect timing.'

The Age

'Ever wondered what happens to the boys from the movie *Jackass* when they grow up? They become oil rig workers. Shit happens, so some of the stuff that Paul Carter and his friends get hit with probably isn't their fault – although sitting at the top of an oil rig derrick during a thunderstorm is probably inviting God to hit you with something. Otherwise most of the madness and mayhem, interspersed with the occasional car or motorcycle accident and totally over the top practical jokes, are clearly all down to Paul. As for the chain-smoking monkeys, pool-playing ferrets and bartending orangutans . . . if the humans are crazy the animals should be too.'

Tony Wheeler, founder of Lonely Planet

'Great two fisted writing from the far side of hell.'

John Birmingham, author

'This is a book for blokes . . . Carter is a kind of modern day Indiana Jones . . . a natural storyteller.'

Sunday Tasmanian

'A unique look at a gritty game. Relentlessly funny and obsessively readable.'

Phillip Noyce, film director

ALSO BY PAUL CARTER

*Don't Tell Mum I Work on the Rigs, She Thinks I'm a
Piano Player in a Whorehouse*

This Is Not a Drill

IS THAT THING DIESEL?

ONE MAN, ONE BIKE AND THE FIRST LAP AROUND AUSTRALIA ON USED COOKING OIL

PAUL CARTER

ALLEN&UNWIN

First published in 2010

Allen & Unwin
83 Alexander Street
Crows Nest NSW 2065
Australia
Phone: (61 2) 8425 0100
Fax: (61 2) 9906 2218
Email: info@allenandunwin.com
Web: www.allenandunwin.com

Cataloguing-in-Publication details are available
from the National Library of Australia
www.trove.nla.gov.au

ISBN 978 1 74175 702 6

Text design by Design By Committee
Typeset by Midland Typesetters, Australia
Printed in Australia by McPherson's Printing Group

10 9 8 7 6

To Lola

CONTENTS

PROLOGUE   1

  1. DERRICK THE MAN   5
  2. COVER YOUR ARSE   14
  3. WHAT COULD POSSIBLY GO WRONG?   20
  4. PANIC FEST   27
  5. BIO WHAT?   48
  6. THE BIKE THE UNIVERSE LANDED   59
  7. BETTY   69
  8. GETTING TO KNOW YOU   79
  9. THERE IS NO PLAN B   90
10. PPPPPP   99
 11. TO ADELAIDE AND BEYOND   109
12. STAGE ONE: GREEN FUEL, WHITE KNUCKLES   125
13. STAGE TWO: SPIDERS   139
14. WALLET   151
15. STAGE THREE: LIFE CYCLE   161
16. STAGE FOUR: FOLLOW THE BLOOD-SPLATTERED
    BRICK ROAD   167
17. THE LONG REACH   189
18. IT ONLY HURTS WHEN I LAUGH   208
19. STAGE FIVE: UNEASY RIDER   229
20. STAGE SIX: NUMB   243
21. STAGE SEVEN: HARDER THAN YOU THINK   248

EPILOGUE   259
ACKNOWLEDGEMENTS   261

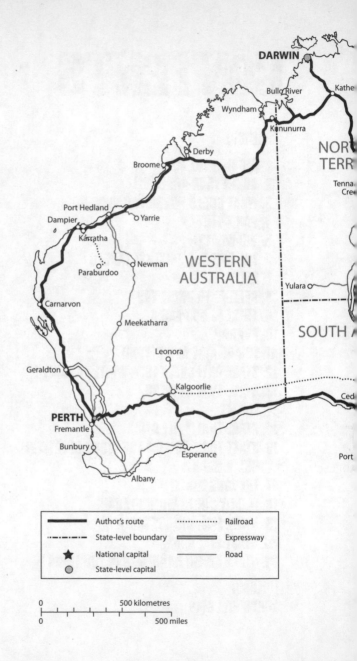

PROLOGUE

My name is mud, or at least it should be. Today I'm taking my cat to the vet, to have him put down. Not, I hear you thinking, the cheeriest way to start a book. But my cat Oswald has reached the end of his days, because his bladder recently reached the end of its days as a functioning organ. There's more cat pee than carpet in the house—it's like the blood in the *Alien* movies, burning little acidic puddles everywhere.

Dead cat walking.

My only regret, I never took him to Vegas.

You will in the course of reading this book—that is,

if I can keep you interested beyond this prologue—hear tales of Oswald my cat, and of my life over the last few years. But before that happens I need to explain how I got to be here in your hands, on this bus, in this toilet, or wherever you like to do your reading.

I'm an oil man, I come from oil parents, and I spent twenty years working on drilling rigs, in sixteen different countries on three different continents, drilling for oil. Dirty, black, stinking, polluting, penguin-clogging, globe-turning, war-inducing, non-renewable, blood-of-Mother-Earth oil. I love it, and it's been very good to me. But now, at the age of 40, I take stock and look back.

From eighteen to 38 I had a ball. So much so I'm amazed I'm not dead. I worked with the same crew of men for fifteen years; they were my brothers. Some were amazing characters who showed me the way, some were sociopaths who should have been institutionalised, and some are now dead. After working and living with them, often in tough locations like jungles or deserts or offshore in the middle of a cyclone, I realise how lucky I am. In 1989 eight guys from my crew died, some in quite horrific circumstances, but I was lucky enough to walk away. Guys I know have had body parts lopped off, or had various things much bigger and heavier than them roll, pinch, crush or land on them while I was standing right there next to them. I have been shot at, held hostage, locked up in a Third World country and locked in the toilet by my own monkey. Many, many times I've found myself in situations that defy reality, but every time I managed to walk away. After twenty years I got spat out by the oilfield rotational life in one piece, my sanity, liver and fingers intact. Why, I have no fuckin idea.

My first book about living the life of an oilfield contractor, *Don't Tell Mum I Work on the Rigs, She Thinks I'm a Piano Player in a Whorehouse*, was published in 2005, my second book *This Is Not a Drill* in 2007, and quite by accident, my publisher tells me I'm an international bestseller. Like everything else in my life, I was in the right place at the right time. This phenomenon continues, as you'll discover if you choose to read on.

Why, I have no fuckin idea.

1 DERRICK THE MAN

'What's in Perth?' Dave Sadler stood in my garage in Sydney leaning against my Kawasaki, scratching his crotch and looking confused.

'Mate, we're moving to WA in two weeks. I've taken a desk job.'

'Oh,' he said. He knew about my promise to my wife, a promise I'd made years ago, that if we ever had kids, I'd stop working offshore on drilling rigs and stay in one place, stay at home and be a father. He knew Clare was six months pregnant, he knew I was worried about finding a stay-at-home job in a city like Sydney, and he knew I would probably move interstate, but he'd wanted to avoid the conversation as much as I did.

'Shit, mate.' He finished his beer. 'I'm going to miss ya.'

Dave had just given me a hand with a new set of exhaust pipes. We'd changed out the baffles, altering the note on a Harley-Davidson XR from a modest rumble to something like King Kong gargling battery acid. Dave grinned as he killed the engine.

I knew I was about to begin a new stage in my life, but I didn't want this one to end. I'd miss our regular motorcycle-maintenance and beer-drinking sessions and blats into the hills. Dave was a motorcycle journalist. We'd met years earlier. For a long time I'd thought motorcyclists in Sydney were a really friendly bunch; every time I was off the rig and belting around the eastern suburbs on my bike I'd get a wave during rush hour on the big lane split into Bondi. Turned out it was Dave every time, just on a different bike each month. When we finally stopped one day in the same place he explained he'd been waving to me for ages. 'Mate, I always had on the same helmet.' I hadn't noticed.

Though I didn't want it to, my time in Sydney was ending. Staying in our tiny flat and rotating out to a different rig every month just didn't fit into our plan now that Clare was pregnant.

We needed a house, with a garden. I needed a normal job, home every night, no more adventures; I knew I could no longer just roll up after a job and jump on my bike and disappear for a few days. It was time to get serious about our future. I had to grow up.

Shortly after that conversation with Dave, Clare and I packed our life into cardboard boxes, I freighted my bikes to a mate's place and had the obligatory fight with the real estate agent over repainting our flat, and a broken stove (it never worked properly anyway, all I ever did was light cigarettes off it). We had already found a great house to rent in Perth through the internet—compared to our tiny flat it was like Graceland. I had a desk job lined up with a drilling tool rental company in Perth. The move went like clockwork.

In Perth, Clare was blissfully happy. She'd wanted to be a wife and a mother since she was old enough to drape a pillow case over her head and pretend she was a bride. Now she was married and pregnant, and had me permanently at home. And when Clare is happy, she bakes. I came home every day from my new job to wonderful dinners and—I kid you not—cherry pie, unquestionably the sluttiest of the pie family. I couldn't believe my luck. After years of offshore galley dining at 'Chucks' in the Third World and then crawling off to a bunk in a four-man room smaller than my broom cupboard and smellier than the toilets in a cheap cigar factory, I was instead wiping whipped cream off my face and curling up each night in a bed like a sprung tennis court, with my gorgeous, pregnant wife; I was looking like one rabid, but very happy—and fat—dog.

Between all the cooking and the eating, Clare was nesting, so we went shopping, collecting all kinds of shiny new baby stuff. Let me tell you about baby stuff: there are strollers, big, fully integrated, multi-function, dual-directional, go-faster-James-Bond ones with better brakes and suspension than my car. Cots that are stronger, more comfortable and bigger than the bunks offshore. In fact, there are whole superstores that supply every baby thing imaginable. We made endless consecutive trips, collecting carloads of stuff that all needed assembling. We got a pram, a cot, and a baby monitor to wiretap our child's room. We even made the obligatory trip to the brand-new, brilliantly designed mega-Ikea store, joining up with hundreds of other shoppers at the bottom of the escalator like migrating salmon. Everyone had their Ikea face on, that 1000-yard stare into the wonders of modern Swedish pre-fabricated, flat-pack laminated furniture. Clare grabbed the brilliantly designed Ikea shopping trolley, the only item they produce that I actually like, and we entered the one-way river of Ikea zombies. Two hours later, the river emerged into a great feeding hangar—with your eyes shut it sounded like you were stepping into a lagoon full of flamingoes at dinner time. We waited in the brilliantly designed holding zone until a JCB deposited five metric tonnes of flat-packed brown cardboard boxes and an Allen key. All this for one very small baby.

With all the new things for the baby and the house we had to make room. Most of our existing furniture was pretty old, predominantly from the 1950s, but it was well made, so it seemed a shame to toss it. Having moved to Perth from Sydney I was used to just dumping unwanted items on the street. Bondi, where we lived, was for all intents and purposes a black hole where entire skiploads full of old junk evaporated overnight. Furniture moves so fast out there that all the homeless cats in Bondi have nothing left to piss on. (Seriously, you could dump a body on the sidewalk in Bondi and some backpacker would fuck off with it and turn it into a coffee table before you could say, 'Whatever happened to Grandpa?' I once left the most diabolical second-hand mattress on the street, just left it propped up against a lamppost. It looked like someone had shot a snuff movie on it. The next day—gone.)

But in Perth, in the refined environs of Nedlands, the items I left out—which I'll have you know were by no means crap—just sat there for weeks. Which left our house marked as the one moved into by trailer trash. Joggers would scowl at me while I watered the front garden; drivers would slow down and point. I found it quite annoying, although eventually I amused myself by standing in our messy front yard in just a pair of tracky pants and a stained wife beater, scratching my back with a toilet brush and belching my name. In the end, though, I had to pay someone to haul the stuff off just to stop us from being run out of the neighbourhood.

There's a strange kind of dynamic lethargy and indifference in Perth. People are almost snobby but not enough to piss you off. New luxury shops are springing up all over the place as the current mining and oil boom has injected billions of dollars into the local economy, lining the pockets of the real estate lucky and the people who work in the right industries. CUBs are popping up like mushrooms—albeit mushrooms with oversized status handbags and Armani sunglasses. CUBs: this was a new term for me—cashed up bogans. Blue-collar guys earning more than Somalia's national debt, and looking to buy new toys.

The family across the road had clearly benefited from the boom years. The dad was in real estate and had recently had all his tats removed. Their house was impressive, two storeys of limestone and marble with a manicured front lawn big enough to host the next Olympics on. Their daughter was around nine, and had more toys scattered over the front yard than I had ever seen when I was her age.

One morning I went outside and a bouncy castle bigger than the flat I grew up in was just sitting on their lawn. I couldn't help comparing it to the toys I'd had at that age.

When I was a lad I had to make do with improvised bits of shit I found on the street or hand-me-downs from my older sister. She hated having to share her toys with me. But hell, whoever said necessity was the mother of invention was onto something. Barbie, with her hair cut off and a texta-applied beard, in clothes made by my mum, made one hell of an action hero. The other kids had the real deal of course, GI Joe, Action Man, Stretch Armstrong, Big Jim, and Steve Austin with his mechanical arm and bionic eyeball. Austin was the best. You could peek out the back of his head through his bionic eye, and that was about as cool as it gets when it's 1979 and you're ten. I did my best to make my sister's former Barbie look manly: I took a bastard file to her boobs, and beefed up her arms with gaffa tape. I ran the edge of a hot knife down her cheek, distorting her right eye and leaving her looking like she'd been through the windscreen of a truck. I renamed her 'Derrick the Man', and convinced the other kids he was special and could breathe fire.

Still, I couldn't compete; one boy had the Evil Knievel action figure—it came with the Harley-Davidson XR750 and a ramp. We would have wars in the backyard, and every time, without fail, Evil would shoot through the air on his bike and save the fuckin day. Steve Austin, Action Man, Big Jim and GI Joe would cheer, while Derrick the Man just stood there looking like a tranny.

Until I put a hot nail through his pursed lips and filled his head up with lighter fluid. The resulting inferno nearly put the lot of us in hospital.

My reverie was broken by a bloodcurdling scream. The little kid from over the road was standing in the street screaming at her parents; listening in, turned out the bouncy castle wasn't the one she wanted. The dad was trying to calm her down, then he spotted me sitting there watching and waved the way you do at a neighbour you don't really know. He smiled, blindingly white teeth, bleached to perfection. My mind tripped and I found myself thinking about kids in West Africa expiring in the dust with perfect complexions and the whitest teeth you have ever seen . . .

I should have gone inside and forgotten about it, but I couldn't. There was a pitch-dark rage building inside me. I wanted to watch that bouncy castle burn. Just as I was thinking I should get the fuck out of there before I said or did something Clare would later bollock me for, the dad wandered over and tried to strike up a conversation.

I was sitting on the weekend paper; our front step was wet from the rain earlier. He made me squint when he smiled. He was clearly just so happy with his stuff: the big house, nice car, his wife, his toys, his kid.

'Are you reading that?' he said, still smiling, pointing at my newspaper.

'Yes,' I replied flatly. 'I have an eye in my anus.'

His smile faded and he asked me what my problem was. My anger deflated. He was right, I was being a jerk. I got up and handed him my paper.

'What happened to your ink?' I gestured towards his forearms.

'Not so good for business, you know?' He shrugged and smiled again, a bit uncertainly.

I smiled back. He once had a young man's tattoos. What now? What images could cover the scars left behind that would accurately capture impending middle age? Precisely how does one illustrate an irritable bowel and mortgage repayments? But I didn't say any of this. Just gave a non-committal wave and wandered inside. I knew I'd been a rude prick. I was missing the rigs, missing the old days, missing those giddy flat-out rides into the hills with Dave. For twenty years I'd been running all over the planet, rig-hopping from one job to the next, completely free, no ties to anyone or anything. Now my crew had moved on and I was in a suburban utopia more imposing and alien than any jungle I'd worked in. I told myself this was the new life that I so desperately wanted, but honestly? It was on the verge of blossoming into a real three-fingered prostate exam.

2 COVER YOUR ARSE

Having over the course of the last year got married, stopped working offshore, knocked up my wife and moved to the 'burbs of Perth, I was now officially middle-aged and boring. Let me tell you how I learned this.

Clare's brother Mathew came to Perth the first week we were there, in his role as manager of a band that was playing a gig in a city club on Saturday night. It was all a bit last minute and rushed but my wife is very tight with her family and it was her only opportunity to see her brother. So, even though she was eight months pregnant, we went along.

We got to the venue, parked out the back, and Matt was there, grinning. He told us the band was a breeze to look after. As well as managing a band, Matt also plays with his own group, The Drugs. The Drugs play hard and party harder. To give you some idea of just how hard, Matt's stage name is Ian Badly. After one of their tours, I once saw Matt with a laminated card around his neck that read: 'My name is Ian Badly. If I am drunk and/or wasted, not making any sense or passed out, I am staying at the Holiday Inn. Please contact our manager on . . .' By contrast, the biggest problem Matt had getting these other guys on stage was dragging them away from their hairdryers and make-up.

Matt is the funniest and most disturbing of all my relatives and in-laws; his sense of humour is sharper than a new razor and equally dangerous. He often has pink streaks in his hair and most of my oilfield mates would assume on first appearance that Matty is gayer than two cocks touching. Matt's short stocky frame and boyish good looks often lead people into making benign assumptions about him, when in fact beneath his good looks and quirky charm is a head space that should have danger signs around it.

The three of us chatted for an hour or so, then the band went on and about a thousand chicks rushed the stage. I wandered to the bar to get a beer; pausing to look into the back of the venue, I saw a group of eight girls staring at me. I smiled, they smiled, and the cock-eyed optimist in my pants shouted up to my brain, 'Yup, you've still got it.' Then one of the girls broke free. She was around twenty, or probably not, and she was wearing a very short skirt and a push-up bra. My balls twitched; it was like a koi pond down there—I was doing my best not to clap.

'So are you with the band?' she asked, thumbing a Bic lighter.

'What makes you think I'm with the band?' There was no way she saw me talking to Matt, I told myself; I have so still got it.

She snorted smoke out. 'Well, you're either someone's dad or you're with the band.'

I was crushed. That's right, I'm thirty-nine. Where's my pregnant wife? What the fuck am I doing here?

On Monday morning I was sitting at my desk considering this same question. What the fuck was I doing there? I was the Rental Tool Manager; I'd been in the job for a week and already I was making quite an impression. The previous Wednesday I sent a quote to a drilling company for a bit of kit called a split bowl. Not a difficult task, and I certainly knew what a split bowl was. Problem was, my business writing skills were not quite on par with my equipment knowledge: I sent them a quote for a split *bowel*. And then I signed off as the Rectal Manager. Oh yeah, I'm the man. The drilling manager responded a few days later; a guy I'd worked with years earlier, he signed off by saying he always knew I was an arsehole.

Simple things that others took for granted mystified me. For example, on my first day the bloke at the next desk emailed me a request. I read it, looked to my left and said, 'Sure, no probs.'

He gave me a sympathetic smile and responded via email, explaining as a footnote that I needed to cover my arse by putting absolutely everything in an email from now on. This struck me as both good advice and a horrible thought. It didn't matter if the person you were talking to nodded and said, 'Yes, I understand, I'll do that today.' No, I had to follow up with an email, get t-shirts printed, and put post-it notes on the wall in front of me to remind myself not to let him forget so that I would have some proof when he *did* forget and so we could assign blame correctly.

What the fuck did we do before email? How did we assign blame? Or was the 'give a fuck' factor just higher then?

How many emails would I have to write, just to cover my arse?

I was not the boss anymore, this was not a drill floor, and my fragile male ego made me want to tell everyone politely just to fuck off. Instead I had to suppress my urge to kick people as they sleepwalked through their day doing just enough not to get fired. There was no work ethic like I was used to. On the rigs, the crew would back each other up in every way. But onshore, in a regular job, I was clearly on my own.

The drilling guys would quickly weed out the weak link in the work chain, or just refuse to go offshore with someone lazy or indifferent—they're too dangerous. Years ago, I was sent to work at a supply base for a month while the rest of my crew went offshore. I was being punished for destroying a hire car—but that's another story. I was on half pay, working seven days a week loading out drill pipe and prepping it for inspection. Buffing tool joints with an angle grinder in the sun for twelve hours a day and being made to work with guys I looked down on was a good head check for me.

That was the first time I experienced the kind of slack, hide-from-the-boss bullshit that made me rage—mostly in the slovenly form of Victor the forklift driver. One morning, I wandered into the workshop, and there was Victor floating around the entrance like a vegetarian turd. He was wearing an orange t-shirt that read 'Drink More Piss'. I vented at him simply because he was there.

'What the fuck are you doing, Vic?'

He looked at me. 'I'm waiting for the Jiffy slut,' he responded matter-of-factly.

'The fuckin what?'

Right on cue the Blue Jiffy Food Company van pulled into the car park.

'That lady is very nice, Vic; don't call her a slut, OK mate?' I said, trying to keep things civil.

But Victor was already mentally inhaling sausage rolls, visibly salivating as he meandered in a Jiffy trance towards the back of the van. He was a cross between Pavlov's dog and Homer Simpson, only more food obsessed. Every day before lunch he devoured two jumbo sausage rolls with extra salt and sauce, then choked down two smokes. Vic's colon must have been the size of the Hindenburg; his gut was so big that his belly still rubbed against the steering wheel even with the seat on the forklift racked back as far as it would go.

Like clockwork, at 10 a.m. the next day he was lurking in the shadows of the workshop entrance like a fat ninja. This time I snuck up on him.

'Who you waiting on, Vic?'

He turned, smiled and grunted, 'The pie mole.'

3 WHAT COULD POSSIBLY GO WRONG?

Nine months into her pregnancy, Clare started to get painful back spasms; she looked like she had been shot in the back with a nuclear submarine. At first I felt helpless, but after talking to her and asking lots of questions I rigged up a rope harness in the garage. Clare would dangle there in among the motorcycles, gently swinging, relief spreading across her face.

The day Clare finally said it was time to go to the hospital—13 December 2007, the day Lola arrived—changed everything for me forever. It was like joining the Mob; I was in for life, no backing out. The fuzzy ultrasound image that I'd stared at in disbelief was about to breathe new life into my corner.

The birth was a lot like being in a Roman Polanski film: confidence seguing into terror, followed by an epidural, followed by an emergency caesarean, followed by a double Scotch. I knew my wife was mentally and physically strong, but Jesus. She comes from a long line of hard-core Catholic working-class ladies; her mother produced five children, in each case working full time until her waters broke, then she mopped the floor, knocked off and walked to the hospital.

I'll spare you the details of the labour, but suffice to say after being an observer I'm sure there must be a special thing that helps women forget the months of pregnancy and the delivery once it's over. I now know for certain that men would never have the balls to nut out a sprog; we would rather have sex with a bear trap. Here's to all the mothers: we men salute you.

Lola was perfect, a mini me: bald, blue eyes, with a breast fixation. Clare says the only reason she looks exactly like me is so I won't eat her. But I was in love, beyond smitten; I could have been the Dean of Smitten at Smitten University. Lola shat on me, threw up on me, peed on me, ate the buttons off my favourite shirt; it was like being in a country and western song, but I didn't care. This, as my fellow parents well know, is the way of the universe.

I struggled with the simple things, like trying to dress her, paranoid that I would snap off a finger or throttle her in an attempt to put on her jumper. Bathing her felt like handling a particularly slippery unexploded bomb, a scenario that made me sweaty and unsure about so much more than just cutting the blue wire.

I felt a wonderful new parental sobriety surround me. Lola had been there for the last nine months, the bulge in Clare's belly; each night I had talked to the bulge about my day. But now—when she was quiet—I had the privilege of talking to her face to face. My life would never be the same again. It was like there was a lamp in my head, and it had always been there, only Lola had just turned it on.

I'd been living the last nine months underwater and now I could suddenly breathe. I was about to turn forty, and finally I felt like I'd come full circle, from a happy-go-lucky arse wrangler, to a semi-functioning wino, to proud father and husband.

We took lots of photos—at first most were a bit reminiscent of Sid and Nancy—and within days whole hard drives were full. Floods of gifts arrived and the house started to look like the Myer baby department during a stocktake sale. My life was becoming textbook white picket fence; it was like living in a Hallmark card. I knew it couldn't last.

Indeed, while home was great, my desk job wasn't improving on closer acquaintance. And the sleep deprivation caused by a new baby didn't help. I came home from work late one Friday, exhausted after a really shit day. On any given Friday someone pivotal would not show up. On this particular day, it fucked me up royally.

We'd received a last-minute order—the only sort there is in the oilfield—and so I had spent the entire day in the pipe yard moving drill pipe from one rack to another, trying to sort out what was good to go. It was a stinking hot summer day, the dust, grease and sweat were staining my shirt, and the whole time I knew there were dozens of other things I had to get done. My mobile went off constantly, the receptionist kept paging me, the paperwork kept piling up; I worked through lunch, then through dinner, and finally left work at 9 p.m.

Pulling into the driveway I could already hear my daughter screaming inside the house. And I was in the car. With the windows up. And the motor still running. I took a deep breath and headed inside.

Clare was sitting on the couch in the living room. The day had been a scorcher, and even at this late hour the house we were renting—an old sprawling 1930s uninsulated heat trap—was stifling. She was lathered in sweat; I had never seen her look so stressed. Lola's screams penetrated my inner brain box like a 9-mm hollow point. Neither of us had the energy to do anything, but I told Clare to give me the baby so she could go and have a shower and take a break. Her response was immediate and vocal.

'The washing machine has flooded the laundry,' she screamed. 'I can't get anything done. Go and fix it!'

In these situations it's better to comply with instructions and just do as you're told, so I went to the shed, got the tools, and within ten minutes the washing machine was sitting on bricks with me lying in dirty, foamy water underneath. Now, I'm no washing machine mechanic, but a scan around with my torch soon revealed that the drain hose was blocked, so I stuck the end of the torch between my teeth, took off the hose clamp and pulled on the hose.

It immediately jerked free, shooting said blockage—a turd consisting entirely of pubic hair and congealed soap—straight into my waiting open mouth. Almost as quickly, I started to vomit. I tried to sit up, but I was under a washing machine, so instead I bashed my vomit-covered face into the side of the drum, leaving me with a deep gash just above my left eye. The large amounts of claret gushing from my new head wound were staunched by winding half a roll of toilet paper round my head.

It wasn't pretty, but some time later I emerged from the laundry, the machine fixed and running, floor mopped, vomit, blood, soap and pubes removed.

My head was throbbing in tune with Lola's screams, which hadn't subsided the whole time I'd been gone. Poor Clare was sitting in exactly the same spot with exactly the same stressed, sweaty expression on her face. I was so hungry I could have eaten dust, but I was far too fearful to ask what was for dinner. I instead suggested again that Clare give Lola to me so she could go and have that shower. This time she gave me a tired smile and passed the baby over. 'What did you do to your head?' she asked.

Lola was wrapped up tightly in a light pink muslin cloth. She was about a three and a half inch outside diameter, two feet long, with a shiny bald purple veiny head sticking out the end. Naturally I thought, 'Wow, she looks just like an erect cock.'

I sprinted into the study where I drew a Jap eye with crayon on Lola's head, tucked her feet into my pants, and re-emerged into the lounge room shouting, 'Hey honey, check this out.'

I stood side-on so Clare could get the full benefit of my genius. Lola was rigid and I was holding her around the waist. 'Get the camera, get the camera!' I was laughing so hard I couldn't see straight. Clare snapped, grabbed the baby and disappeared back into the bathroom, slamming the door behind her.

Sometime later they reappeared: baby fast asleep, Jap eye removed. Wife was weird-calm. She sat down next to me on the couch, where I was nervously channel-surfing. Without looking at me, Clare spoke in that slightly deeper voice that women use when they really disconnect, and are about to lift cars or kill you with a blunt instrument.

'Don't ever make cock jokes using your daughter as a prop, OK?'

Months later at a public speaking event a bloke asked me if I had learned anything since becoming a father. In front of fifteen hundred people I went blank, then said, 'Don't ever make . . .'

4 PANIC FEST

Not used to being so housebound, previously simple matters—like getting myself around the world at short notice—became surprisingly complicated. In one particular case, I had difficulty leaving the state.

As you'll likely have gathered by now, as well as having a full-time job, I'm also a part-time writer. And one of the things that happens when you're a writer is you get invited to speak at writers' festivals. I had done three; no matter how many times I do it, I still freak at the thought of talking to large groups of people. Then along came the Melbourne Writers' Festival. Even the invitation letter was flash. It's one of the premier writing events in the country—how the hell did I get an invite? I promptly phoned my publisher, who confirmed that I was indeed on the billing. So naturally I responded telling them I'd be delighted and thank you very much for thinking of me. Months later I got an information pack from the festival organisers, containing my flight itinerary, hotel reservations, books by the other authors attending, and information on where in Melbourne to get everything from a bikini wax to a good cappuccino.

When the festival dates rolled around Clare was visiting her family in Sydney with eight-month-old Lola. She phoned me the day before I was due to leave for Melbourne, asking if I had remembered to get her car registered. I had purchased Clare a small hatchback just before she left for Sydney, and of course I had completely forgotten to register it. If I didn't drop what I was doing at work and get to the licensing centre pronto, there would be all kinds of shit as a consequence, so I raced out the door and drove to the nearest one, took a number from the machine and sat in the packed waiting room looking at the big red digital numbers clicking over from 28 to 19998.

Several hours later my number appeared and I approached a spotty bored kid with ink all over his hands. He was however very helpful and explained that in order to register Clare's car I would have to give up my New South Wales licence, which he would cancel, then he would give me a Western Australian licence, and then I could register the car. So I handed over my Sydney licence, and he gave me this shitty interim piece of paper, as it takes a week to make a plastic licence in WA. I folded it up and stuck it in my wallet, walked out and rang Clare to tell her everything was sorted and wasn't I organised.

The next morning I woke up nervous; I had packed the night before but I double-checked everything. Hours went into thinking about what I was going to wear for my appearance on stage. I don't usually worry about such things, but at this event I was going to be in the sort of company that makes me anxious. People I've read and admire; gifted, intelligent, articulate writers, like the brilliant Clive James and John Clarke, who would no doubt be wondering what I was doing there. People who would think I'd feel overdressed if I was wearing a belt.

As I made last-minute shoe-change decisions, I paused to calm the fuck down. This is not that big a deal, I told myself, it's just fifteen minutes on stage. I think I know what I'm going to talk about, I know what I'm going to wear, and besides, when I get there we'll have a nice long meeting on who will go first and all that good stuff, so just relax and take your time.

I made myself a cup of tea and sat on the porch for a moment. My cat fronted up from inside a nearby bush and sat directly in front of me, smiling. Oswald is pretty much an outdoor cat; he's scarred from a million fights, and his face is contorted in a permanent scowl thanks to a stroke he suffered a few years ago. He's deaf, his left ear is completely split, his tail has multiple fractures, he's pissed more blood, drank more drain water, and lived through more attempts on his life than most people I know. But he's smart, very smart. I think he's even got his own website.

Oswald spent months checking me out from a safe distance before he decided he was my friend. At night I would see his reflective eyes watching me intently from under a bush or car, sometimes from the roof. Now he knows me as an animal lover and we have quiet moments on the porch together.

He wanders up and growls at me. His cat voice turned into a low rasp years ago; he sounds like a pack-a-day cat. I give him the odd treat, and he forgets himself and thinks he's human, rolls over and shows me his beer gut so I will make a fuss of him.

The family opposite us have a likable but stupid rottweiler, one of those bounding, relentless, totally undisciplined dogs that just does whatever enters its melon head. You know, piss on the car, eat the child, fuck that rubbish bin, rub your arse on the carpet. Oswald and I were enjoying our quiet moment when the rottweiler saw us sitting there on the porch and launched itself away from his owner across the street, coming at us full tilt, its tongue slapping the side of its head. Oswald sensed something was amiss. His head swivelled in the direction of the driveway where 200 pounds of mind-numbingly thick dog was hurtling towards us at breakneck speed.

The dog was ten feet away when it suddenly put the brakes on, skidding to a stop only inches from Ossy. He was barking madly, his spit flying into the cat's face. Oswald didn't move a single muscle, just gave the rottweiler the dead-eye stare. The dog looked completely confused: wasn't it in the cats' contract that Oswald had to shit a brick and run like fuck? But Ossy just turned his head back to me, looking bored. Utterly nonplussed, the dog started running in wild circles, barking randomly, until his owner came down my driveway apologising and dragged the dog off.

Here was an old cat showing me the way: he had just faced down a demented rottweiler and casually fallen asleep. All I had to do was picture the audience as demented rottweilers, naked demented rottweilers, and I'd be fine.

My phone rang; it was my publisher making sure I was ready to go.

I called a taxi and stood in the driveway. I've stood in the driveway a thousand times waiting for a cab to take me to the airport. This time it was not to an end destination on the other side of the world that involved a drilling rig in some swamp. This time it was as a writer. Me, a writer; I still can't believe it.

Perth Domestic Airport is always busy. I joined the queue to check in. My turn arrived and I handed over my ticket.

'Where are we off to today?' The check-in guy faked a smile.

'Melbourne.' I faked one back.

'Right, Mr Carter, I'll need to see photo ID please.'

My hand automatically went to my pocket and then I froze, pulling that face you make when you know you're stuffed. The interim paper licence came out anyway. I showed him the formal invitation letter; I pleaded with him. He pulled the face you make when you don't really give a fuck. The APEC Conference was about to start in Sydney, a delegation of some of the planet's most important decision-makers—and George W. Bush—were about to fly in, so the security protocols required that everyone checking in for a flight needed to have current valid photo ID.

'Sorry,' he smirked, 'I don't make the rules.'

I was livid. Right, I thought, think fast. I ran to the taxi rank, jumped into the first cab and looked into the face of an ancient Indian man with glasses thicker than George W. Shit, I thought, this is going to be like *Driving Miss Daisy* all the way to my house.

'Get me to my house and back here as fast as you can, mate, and I'll look after you,' I said.

George hammered it. I was doing the right foot into the invisible brake thing all the way home. There was no way I was going to get back in time to make my flight, but there was another one departing in a little over an hour. It was the only flight left that could possibly get me there in time—and it would be tight.

I booked it on my mobile while George snaked in and

out of traffic mumbling to himself, constantly pushing his glasses back up on his nose with his index finger. By the time we turned into my street I was starting to feel confident; George had done a sterling job.

'What number?' he asked, but I was staring in shock, my heartbeat had doubled. 'Oooh, there's a fire,' he casually pointed out.

'Stop the car,' I yelled at him. We pulled up in front of my house—my rental house, currently on fire. Neighbours had gathered on the lawn, peering through the front window. Flames were visible and smoke was billowing out.

I ran to the front door fumbling with my keys while the neighbours flashed their whiter than white teeth. 'We called the fireys,' they said. I suppressed the urge to run straight through the kitchen and into the study. No doors in the house were closed and smoke was filling the house from our high ceiling down to head level. I could see into the study from the kitchen; my desk was burning, as was the carpet underneath it, and half my bookshelf. Right, I thought, think faster. Working on drilling rigs, every two years we would do a firefighting course. First we'd practise assessing hypothetical situations and decide the best way to deal with all kinds of different fires, and then we'd spend the rest of the day setting things on fire and putting the theory into practice. After all these years, my first time ever fighting a fire, and I didn't even have time to enjoy it. Shit.

Propped up against the wall by the kitchen door was a nine-kilo dry-powder, big fuck-off industrial fire extinguisher. I grabbed it, pulled the pin, and pointed the nozzle at the bread bin to test it. The corner of our kitchen bench, the bread bin, the toaster, the kettle and a revolting embroidered hanging thing that said 'Clare's Kitchen' were instantly covered in white powder. Yup, it worked. I turned to my study and let fly.

The fire was out before the extinguisher was empty. My passport sat in the top left-hand drawer of my desk. As I pulled it out I heard the fire truck roll up outside. My heart was pounding and I was sweating like a pig. I shoved the passport into my hip pocket and ran out.

On the way out I passed the firemen, the real estate agent and the neighbours, still standing on the porch.

'You got keys?' I said to the worried-looking agent.

'You got insurance?' he replied.

The taxi driver sat there behind the wheel, engine still running. I jumped in and started doing a pantomime for 'get me back to the airport'. He couldn't believe I was just going to leave.

'But what about your house, my friend?'

'Just go,' I snapped.

'Don't you want to change your shirt?'

'No, just go.'

'Did you just use a fire extinguisher?'

'Yup.'

'You know that was very dangerous. What if you inhaled smoke and collapsed?'

'Airport.'

'Yes, I know, you want to go back to the airport. It must be a very important meeting you are going to then.'

'Yup.'

'Do you want me to take the tunnel or go through the city?'

'JUST FUCKING GO.'

George's finger shot up and shoved his glasses back up on his nose and we took off like a rocket. My phone rang. It was the real estate agent: the fire was well and truly out. Thank Christ for that, I thought, imagining the alternative, searching for a way to make myself feel better. All those years of working on the rigs, with endless flights, hundreds of charters, choppers, donkeys, commercial airliners—you name it, I caught it. I had only missed one check-in in twenty years. This time I was lucky I'd missed that flight. The agent was very understanding and said we would get everything sorted out in a couple of days when I got back from Melbourne.

I sat back, trying to relax, looking at my watch every few minutes. There were just too many variables. I had stacked things in my head the way you do when you're confronted with too much to deal with and none of it is really under your control. I stank, sweat was running down my back, my hands were sticky. Meanwhile George continued to drive like a maniac, and we pulled up at the terminal almost before I'd gathered my thoughts. He popped the boot. I slapped two green ones down on his waiting hand and he beamed. 'Good luck to you.'

I had arrived just in time to make the second flight. I couldn't believe it. Skipping the long queue I ran up to the guy at the desk. Same guy, same expression. He even said, 'Where are we off to today?'

'Melbourne.' I slid my passport across the counter to him.

He looked at it for a moment, then looked at me with a mixture of pity and contempt. 'This is expired, Mr Carter.'

My face must have dropped a couple of feet. 'What?' I grabbed it and yes, I had picked up the wrong one. When you get a new passport the government sends back your old one as well, but because it's cancelled they cut off a corner. I stood there for a moment looking at my photo, the top right-hand corner of my head chopped off. How had I missed that?

'Look, you can see it's me,' I said, holding the invitation letter above my face to block out the same area, but it was pointless.

'Sorry, I don't make the rules.' He faked a sympathetic smile and waved up the next person.

I went back outside the terminal and stood there for a moment, getting myself together. I've managed to get myself into and out of some remote corners of the globe, often really shitty parts of the Third World, sometimes countries where civil war was raging, but I couldn't get it together to get out of Perth to go to a writers' festival. I was shaking with anger, but there was nothing to be done; I'd blown it. At least the house hadn't burned down. All I could do was phone the festival organisers and let them know I would be a no-show.

After I made the call, I looked over to the cab rank; there was George reading the paper. The thought of getting in that cab again was too much to bear and I found myself wandering back into the terminal, towards the airport shop. The airport shop where they sell books, books with the author's photo on the jacket . . . motherfucker. I broke into a sprint, grabbed the first book of mine I could see on the shelf, stood in the queue feeling like a dick for buying my own book, then ran back to check-in guy and thrust it under his nose while people in the check-in queue protested. 'What the fuck?'

I ignored them.

'Excuse me, dickhead.' A deep voice spoke close behind me. I turned and the guy stopped mid-speech. No doubt I looked like your stock-standard bald, angry, control-seeking narcissist who's in receipt of some kind of mental benefit. Our eyes met. He took in the stench of a house fire mixed with dry-powder extinguisher, mixed with sweat, mixed with my best fuck-off look, and he took a step back.

I turned around to the check-in guy, who was studying the jacket photo. 'OK, Mr Carter, here's your boarding pass, good luck.' This time he showed teeth.

'Thank you.' I had five minutes. 'Thank you.' I ran towards the security section. 'Thank you,' I yelled over my shoulder.

Sitting in the departure lounge I felt worse than before I made the check-in. Now I had to phone the festival back and tell them I was coming after all. Hearing their confusion, I could tell they were convinced I was an idiot. Finally we boarded. I tried to relax. A quarter of an hour went by, then another. If we didn't push back from the terminal in the next five minutes I wasn't going to make it. If we got underway now, and landed on time, then I had just fifteen minutes to get from the airport to the stage. Christ. I turned my phone on and dialled the only man I knew who could get me from the airport to the festival at light speed. James Ward was my only hope.

James is an interesting guy, affable, funny, in his mid thirties and already the manager of the Supercar Club. He has at his disposal a frightening array of ridiculously fast and exotic sports cars, as well as the necessary driving skills to put a fast car into low orbit.

I'd met him a few months earlier, when a TV crew was in the process of casting the presenters for the Aussie version of the British motoring television show *Top Gear*. Out of the blue they'd called and asked me to audition.

'But I'm not a car guy,' I said, but apparently that didn't matter.

The next day I was on a flight to Sydney, and from there to a small town in rural New South Wales via a minibus. I met James on that bus. From the get-go I was the guy in that group who didn't know about cars. That is to say, yes, I'm a car lover; yes, I know as much as any regular guy who dreams of owning a fully restored 1966 Fastback Mustang, but the others were all walking auto savants who could rattle off every conceivable detail about any car. 'Mate, the GTO was faster than the ABC coz the '76 model had the blah blah plugged into the thingy, blah, blah, blah, blah . . .' was all I heard after the first hour. You can imagine the amount of testosterone in the room, ten guys in heated 'pick me' mode, every last one of them a dedicated car lover.

'Paul, what do you think of my new Ford Blah?' they'd ask.

'Very nice,' I'd say, while another guy jumped in with: 'I've got one, but what about their move over to trans blah, blah . . .' Each question posed with a serious expression, as they tried to feel out exactly how much I don't know about cars. 'What colour is it?' I would respond. Another asked me what I thought about V6 compared to V8 and I told him I preferred apple juice. They must have hated me.

So James and I drank all their single malt, and bonded; James didn't care either.

We drove about in go-karts, racing each other while the decision-makers recorded everything. All I managed was some very average drink-driving, ending in a fairly unspectacular crash. The whole experience was lots of fun, but in the end they chose their presenters and the rest of us sobered up and went back to our regular jobs. James and I stayed in touch, and I'm glad we did. Now I was about to ask him for a huge favour.

He picked up the phone when I rang and without hesitation said, 'No worries, mate, I'll be out the front waiting.' As I turned off my phone and the aircraft finally pushed back, hope flickered alive once again. During the flight I pondered my situation. Why was this so hard? It wasn't like we were trying to breed pandas here, all I had to do was get up and go to the airport for fuck's sake.

The aircraft touched down bang on time in Melbourne; I had no check-in luggage so I bolted for the exit. Hitting the outer doors I spotted James instantly, leaning against a brand-new white Maserati GranTurismo.

Bingo. This was going to be fun, I thought as I ran up. I started thanking him and apologising, but all he said was: 'Jump in.'

I dropped into the low-slung car like you'd slide into a warm bath after a hard day. James took off like we'd just robbed a bank, concentrating totally while making polite conversation. I tried not to look frantic as we passed other cars as if they were standing still. 'How's Lola doing?' James asked casually, taking the Italian V8 from a low growl to a fuel-injected feeding frenzy as he pointed my great white hope towards two giant semitrailers and shot out the minuscule gap between them like an Exocet missile.

'Oh, she's fine, mate.' Time slowed down. I think a little pee came out. I was pushed back into the ample black leather, feeling like a bum in a dinner suit, mesmerised by the number of buttons and dials on the dash.

If we had passed a cop, there would have been just enough time for them to report a UFO. James chatted calmly about everything from politics to soap operas as if he was driving the Popemobile sedately through Rome, not tearing down the Tullamarine Freeway at a million miles an hour. If I had been driving that car we would have ended up vaporised in the grille of a semitrailer full of bridge parts. Or the cops would have nailed me, and what would I have told them? After the day I'd had, I would have welcomed getting arrested. I could have popped open the glove box, and shown the officers the scarf I was knitting or given them a list of the top ten movies that made me cry. Jesus. I needed a tall glass of 'Harden The Fuck Up': there was no backing out now.

If the Nobel Prize Foundation gave out awards for driving, James would have won that day. It was like being on the set of *The Transporter*, but without the guns. We banked hard and darted into an exit. I glanced down at my watch. I had two minutes. 'Don't worry, mate, I'll get you there,' he said in that confident I-could-do-this-shit-for-a-living kind of way. Sure enough, he made it; I owed him one.

My goodbyes were fast. I had already undone the seat belt, and I sprang from the low GT as soon as he pulled up outside one of many entrances to the theatre. It was one of those utterly confusing modern buildings; I had no idea if I was at the right door or even the right building. Adrenalin forced me to run inside, my head darting from left to right as I looked for a magic arrow to point me in the right direction.

A young woman came around the corner in a festival t-shirt wearing a headset and carrying a clipboard, so I grabbed her. 'Hi, I'm supposed to be on stage,' I blurted out.

She scanned the clipboard. 'What's your name?' I told her and bang, we were off: down the hall, up some stairs, down some stairs, through a backstage corridor. I could hear a lot of people settling in on the other side of the wall, and nerves started pulling at my gut.

She stopped and motioned towards a small set of stairs that had to lead to the stage. 'Go out and take your seat,' she said, looking firm.

I stood there for a moment trying to gather my wits. As I took the stairs, time slowed down again; I rounded the corner and there they were, the writers, looking over their glasses at me the way parents observe other people's kids. To my right sat many hundreds of paying members of the general public. I looked like shit on a stick. I sat down in the free seat, sweat making its horribly dank and smelly way down my back.

Suddenly I was being introduced. Shit, I was the first cab off the writers rank today—perfect. I'd thought I'd get the chance to sit down for a few minutes and try to remember what the fuck I had planned to say to these people, but now there was polite applause. Finding my feet, I confidently strode over to the podium, smiling out at the bright lights. I cleared my throat, thanked the festival for inviting me, thanked the members of the audience for coming, and then I went completely blank.

I decided to explain why I looked like shit, and of course I ended up telling the story of my day so far. I had fifteen minutes to speak and it took fifteen minutes to tell the story. I didn't talk about books, or writing, or anything to do with literature. But I did explain that I am indeed the guy who manages to get himself in all kinds of shit just by getting up in the morning. They loved it, thank God.

After the session we all went to the green room where speakers were supposed to wait before going on, and had a drink. On the way I discovered that there was an area outside the green room where we each had a desk set up with our names on a little card, so audience members and festival-goers could buy a book from the bookstore and take it over to the author to sign or write obscenities in, etc. At the end of the row of desks was my name, and a queue of people all holding books. I wandered up as the staff ripped open boxes, pulling out copies of a book by Professor Paul Carter. 'Um, that's not me,' I said, pointing at the pile on the table.

'What?' said the young guy unpacking the books.

'This isn't my work,' I said. I confess, for a moment I thought about just sitting down and signing them.

'Oh, I'm so sorry, we'll get it sorted out.' He grabbed the books and disappeared, leaving me in front of an ever-lengthening line of people.

To my right I could see all the other authors making polite small talk and doing their best signatures on huge piles of books around them. More and more people filtered into the courtyard. It was the entire cast and crew of the Melbourne literary scene; there were pearls and lots of air-kissing. The word 'darling' skipped across lips and reverberated as frequently as 'fuck' used to on the drill floor.

I saw a familiar face in the crowd: not someone I knew, someone I recognised. He got a bit closer. It was Geoffrey Rush, the actor, and he was working his way around the courtyard. Wow, I thought, I'm going to get to meet him. My books had turned up—perfect. I started chatting and signing, all the while closely monitoring Mr Rush's progress towards my table.

It was all going very well: the people waiting for me to sign their books were all very nice, the wine was very nice, the gentle tones of civilised conversation broken by the occasional laugh were all just very nice. The sun was shining and birds sang from trees nearby.

That's when I heard it, a rough voice that could have come straight from the oilfield, shattering the peace and my sensation of wellbeing. 'Oi, are you Paul Carter?'

Turning to my right I saw a six-foot, 300-pound, slightly drunk man with full-sleeve tats and wearing a VB t-shirt with sauce stains down the front, eyeballing me through more facial hair than I thought it was humanly possible to grow.

'Yup.' I smiled. I think he smiled back.

'I fuckin loved your book, hey.'

'Thanks, mate.' Just past his left shoulder I saw another familiar face approaching through the crowd; this time it was someone I knew.

'M'name's Dwayne hey.' My new fan stuck out a massive hairy hand. I dived my hand into his, making full contact with his upright thumb, enabling me to get a firm grip and shake. I looked him in the eye; he was pissed. I darted a look at Mr Rush—his entourage was getting awfully close—at my friend, now waving and bounding through the crowd towards me, and then back to Dwayne, who was still talking at me.

'Lemme shout you a beer, mate,' he said, raising his other hand. Only then did I notice the stubbie neck just visible through the furry knuckles.

'Cheers, Dwayne,' I said. 'I'll just finish up here, mate, and meet you at the bar in half an hour.'

At that moment, my friend appeared next to Dwayne.

'Hi, Bruce.' I hugged him and we shook hands. Bruce is a truly gifted man, he's a very talented writer and filmmaker, a gentleman in every way.

'Why does this stuff always happen to you?' Bruce was laughing—clearly he'd heard about my day so far. Mr Rush was now ten feet away.

I introduced Dwayne to Bruce and they regarded one another carefully—it was like worlds colliding. Bruce, ever the gentleman, politely smiled and got his manicured hand crushed by Dwayne, who defaulted back to beer.

'I'll shout yas both a beer.'

Mr Rush was now just a few feet away and getting closer. Bruce was enjoying himself. 'Have you read Paul's books?' he asked Dwayne.

Dwayne looked at Bruce's perfect attire, his neat, clean, personable aura, and spoke loud enough for half the courtyard to hear him. 'Mate, I'm just like him. I know what it's like to work for a living hey, not like all these cunts.'

The second Dwayne dropped the C bomb, Mr Rush turned on his heel and melted back into the crowd.

Bruce was loving it. 'Go on, Pauli, have a beer with him.' He nudged me with his elbow and gestured towards Dwayne's hand. 'Look, he's got a traveller.'

Dwayne looked at Bruce. I looked at Bruce. 'He's got a what?' I started to worry.

'You know, a traveller.'

At this point Dwayne stepped forward, and with his beard almost touching Bruce's face said, 'Mate, a beer you walk around with is generally referred to as a *roadie*; a *traveller* is when you crack a fat on public transport.'

'Oh.' Bruce nodded. 'I'll try to remember that.'

Dwayne stepped back, took a long swig of his beer and regarded the two of us. You could almost hear the penny drop: it was like a thought bubble appeared above Dwayne's head that read, 'Oh, they're a gay couple. Paul Carter's a poofter.'

This could not have panned out any better for me. Bruce registered all this and kindly helped me to embrace the horror by placing a hand on my shoulder. That cemented the picture for Dwayne, who got out of there so fast you would have thought his hair was on fire.

5 BIO WHAT?

Not long after the writers' festival, I started a new job in Perth with an oilfield supply firm, working in a small office not too far from home. The job was perfect; the boss was just like me, he'd worked in the field for years, and everyone we did business with was pretty much from the old school. Most of our business dealings were conducted over a single malt at lunch, very civilised.

By this time, I'd settled down a bit. My wife was amazing; my child was amazing, they made me dizzy with contentment. I actually enjoyed my job and we had purchased a house that ticked every box. I would stand in the power tool section at the hardware store, envisaging potential backyard projects. On weekends I pruned hedges and mowed the lawn. I made polite conversation with my neighbours wearing a silly hat to keep the sun off my bald head. I even got to know the postman—I never ever thought I'd know the postman.

After kicking and screaming all the way from the rig for the last twelve months, I had crossed over into the next stage of my life. Well, you can't stay in a bad mood forever. I'd turned into the grey man living the middle-class dream—there was even a white picket fence around my house. I bolstered my pension plan and life insurance, I stopped smoking, and before the rebellious voice in my head could say, 'Hey, what the fuck?', it was my fortieth birthday and I was in bed by ten.

Christ, I was middle-aged and happy about it.

For my birthday I got the regulation socks and jocks, a gift voucher for the hardware store, and a copy of *Long Way Round*, the documentary series on Ewan McGregor and Charley Boorman's epic motorcycle ride. When I did finally get the chance to sit down and watch it I discovered instead Lola's *Finding Nemo* disc inside, my sixteen-month-old daughter having put my DVD into one of the many cases piled up on the floor.

Whereas in my old life I used to play beat the clock on every job, I had even stopped marking time. Despite this, the year had blown by faster than I'd ever experienced before. There were reminders of what I now looked back on as my old life; for example, my friend Erwin, who still lived at a pace I couldn't comprehend from the 'burbs and was still working offshore. He'd come home to Perth on a crew change, and within 24 hours of arriving he'd ride his motorcycle over to our house and demand a long ride into the hills.

Erwin was my mentor: we had spent many years rig-hopping all over the world together. He's a larger than life character, he has the light around him—you know, anything could happen and he would walk away without so much as a scratch. Our friendship had literally kept me in one piece for the better part of fifteen years; I would have been eaten alive by the oilfield without his guidance. If Mother Nature wasn't trying to kill us there always seemed to be something else that was. The first time I went up in the derrick—that's the big steel mini-Eiffel Tower on the rig—it was Erwin who taught me how not to fall, get crushed, or cut any limbs or fingers off. Believe me, over the years a great many men have hurt themselves up there. If it were not for his patience and skill I probably wouldn't have the digits to sit here and type this.

These brief two-wheel interludes with my old friend became very important to me. Time spent on my bike put me in a mindset that I just couldn't replicate any other way. When Erwin and I got tired, we'd stop and rest and I caught up on all his latest adventures.

Even though I was getting used to life at home, something was not quite right. Maybe it was turning 40; maybe it was a lingering sense of loss, knowing that I had departed a life I had loved for twenty years and could never go back. I still missed being on the rigs. It was always fun working and hanging out with my crew; I had never laughed so hard or been so scared in my life. Or maybe what I missed was the sense in those days that adventure was a thing that just happened, without any planning or preparation, just random spontaneous life getting in the way.

In the weeks after my birthday I started to realise that I couldn't go on in the same way that I'd been living for the last year or so; I just wanted more from my life. And when I say more, I'm not talking about material goods. The arrival of Lola and the profound and all-encompassing impact of being a father had helped drown out all that chatter and white noise and worries that can make us slaves to our possessions. It's funny how your kids change your priorities overnight. So long as Clare and Lola were alright, you could set fire to all our shit (I had a bit of experience at that now) and I wouldn't bat an eyelid. I used to worry about my stuff, my special things, but not anymore. Doesn't matter if it's something really nice or valuable, in the end you're just the custodian of it for a while, then someone else gets it anyway. No, this restlessness was just about adventure.

The highway sat there out the window, waving a dusty invitation at me through the heat haze. Back in Sydney I had been able to indulge myself on my days off. If the urge got to me, all I had to do was wander into my garage and get on a bike. Not just a bike, an escape into a mindset of corners, faster each time; a heightened sense of awareness that blanks your troubled mind and focuses it on one thing only: the ride. No responsibilities, no life insurance, no five-year plan. It's not just a bike, it's a get-into-jail card, it's an unlicensed weapon and a fat bank guard, it's whatever you want it to be, as fast as you like.

I would leave the city and head south, to Araluen; sometimes I would just keep going, stopping when I got hungry or tired, buying clean jocks and socks in some small town, throwing the old ones in a motel bin, getting drunk with strangers and ending up in Melbourne. I missed those days, before I was a grown-up.

At the halfway mark during one of our rides to nowhere in particular, I looked over a roadhouse table at Erwin and announced, 'I'm going to ride my bike around Australia.'

He finished his mouthful of steak sandwich and beamed. 'When are we leaving?'

'How about now?' Obviously I was joking, but there was a time when that was exactly what we'd have done.

Erwin looked at me thoughtfully. 'You watched that *Long Way Round* DVD I gave you for your birthday?' he asked.

'No, not yet.' I was looking at the bikes in the car park.

During the ride home the idea solidified in my head. I thought, I'm not done, I'm nowhere near done. Somehow, I was going to get the time off work, talk Clare into giving me a leave pass, and get to have my cake and eat the bastard too. The thought sat there in my head, bobbing about like a crouton in my brain soup for weeks—and it *was* soup, strained through months of paperwork, tender documents, pre-qualification questions. The detritus of business was weighing down my itchy feet, a paperweight of increasing responsibilities, increasing business lunches and my increasing waistline—all of which pushed me to broach the idea with Clare.

My wife, flat out dealing with motherhood, which is in itself much harder and more draining than anything I'm ever tasked with during the day, listened patiently while I blurted out my idea. I was nervous: I knew it was a big ask.

She surprised me. Apparently, Clare had been waiting for me to do this for a while. She said she knew it was only a matter of time before sitting behind a desk and living in Lego Land would turn my life into a cage with golden bars.

'You're going to write about this, right?' she asked me. What can I say, she knows me well.

'Well yeah, why not?' I replied, wondering where she was going with this.

'Honey, anyone can get on a conventional motorcycle and ride it around Australia. You should find a machine that's different.'

The more I thought about it, the more it made sense. After all, Ewan McGregor and Charley Boorman had punched out two books and two TV series about riding around the world. (Which reminded me, I still hadn't found my copy of their DVD yet.) Motorcycle travel/ adventure has been done to death.

So, how would I jump on a bike and have an adventure without replicating what's been done before? I knew I couldn't get anywhere near what those guys did. Ewan McGregor is a movie star, they had limitless funding, an army of people in support, and the ability to make shit happen on their custom-designed, top-flight BMWs. And that's the point: I'm about as far removed from their end of the spectrum as humanly possible. Whatever I did, it had to be different.

And then a light bulb went on over my head. I couldn't believe I hadn't thought of this earlier. Enter Mr Greg Quail, aka Quaily—an old mate, a prince among men. Greg runs a successful television production company based in Sydney; he's animated and insightful, but above all, when he's armed with an idea he likes, he won't let go. He's like a greyhound chasing after a stuffed rabbit. Earlier in the year, one of Greg's staff, Warwick Burton, had called me to discuss the idea of Quail Television making a show about a ride on a bio-diesel motorcycle. I had thought it was brilliant, and perfect for me: I'm the oil guy—what else should I ride but a bike that runs on bio-diesel, environmentally friendly fuel?

It had sounded redeeming, and at the time, was a nice alternative to going back offshore. But the idea never made it past conception, and I'd put it out of my mind.

Now, when I reminded her, Clare said I should call and find out how far Warwick got with his research. I practically knocked her over in my rush to get to the phone.

But Greg and Warwick didn't have good news for me; apparently the TV networks in Australia, while interested and enthusiastic about the concept, thought the idea was too expensive to make. The networks are generally more interested in something 'reality'-based, something that's cheaper to put on the telly. You know, 'Find My Bogan' or 'World's Silliest Bogan', or a group of people trying to lose weight, or dance or sing or cook or renovate another fucking house, or a bunch of celebrities between gigs dissecting the news on a panel. That kind of stuff is cheap and very simple to produce. But above all, it's what we want to watch at prime time, isn't it? Not a bloke riding a motorcycle around, especially if he's not overweight and not trying to dance, sing, cook, renovate a house or find a long-lost degenerate alcoholic sibling.

I just don't understand the way the TV game works. Greg is a good mate, and whenever I'm in Sydney or he's in Perth we get together and, as mates do, we discuss work. But I have neither the patience nor the ability to try to comprehend how Greg gets an idea for a show, makes a pilot or reel and then sells it to a network.

Sounds simple, doesn't it? Well, as far as I can make out, quantum physics is simpler. Essentially, the 'bio-diesel bike ride around Australia' idea was too much of a hard sell, and Greg had to shelve it.

However, I was only concerned with the ride, and Greg was only too happy to pass on the info they'd compiled on the bio-diesel motorcycles currently available. Armed with Greg and Warwick's research, I started my own hunt for information. There are several bio-diesel motorcycles commercially available in the world, but none of them are for sale in Australia. I found a great bike made in America, another in Holland, one in Japan, and a really good one in Germany fabricated by a former uber-lieutenant from Porsche who had packed in his job and started building bio-fuel bikes. (Germany, I learned, has over 1600 bio-diesel fuel stations.) His bike was perfect and completely capable of doing the ride. But no matter where in the world I found a bike I liked, I couldn't get a compliance plate on it or get it legally registered and insured so I could ride the bastard round Australia.

This mad hunt for bikes went on for months. Several times I came close to nailing it, but in the end, as everything does, it boiled down to two basic problems: time and money. I had planned to set off on the first of September to get the best weather and wind direction, heading east. But it was May and I was running out of options. As far as I could make out, getting the Batmobile for a blat around Australia would be a whole lot easier than getting hold of a bio-diesel bike. I could see why no one had done it before. I wanted to be the first rider to circumnavigate the country on a motorcycle running on used cooking oil, but good old-fashioned bureaucracy was pulling the rug out from under me.

Another potentially big hurdle was that I would also need to convince my employers to let me go and do 'the thing with the bike', as it would become known.

My immediate boss, Craig Voight, is based in Queensland; like all the other area managers, I report to him, and Voighty in turn reports to Peter West—Westy—who reports to the owner of the company. I had to ask Voighty first; if he said yes then I could ask Westy (I know it's getting silly, but the area manager in Adelaide is called Rossy). Craig was as calm and laid-back as ever; I, however, was nervous. I was a new employee, I'd been there just on a year. But all he said was: 'OK mate, run it past Westy.'

I'd known within minutes of meeting Peter West that he was a character. He stands out in a room, not just because he's a big man but because he has presence. If Westy was at the obligatory Thursday night oilfield drinks, then I knew the conversation would be good. Westy looks like he should be either a cop or a crim: he has that face; he's seen life, and people listen when he speaks. His hair is cropped short and neat, and he's always in a suit. But he can, when he's in the right mindset, carry himself in a way that makes you think he's just come from his millionth parole hearing. He has the demeanour of a man who's at peace with himself, but he also gives off the vibe that he's capable of anything. In reality, though, he is a gentle man who needs intolerable provocation to become violent, and you always know exactly where you stand with him.

Bearing in mind all that makes Westy Westy, I walked into his office one morning and asked him if he'd have a problem if I took off for three months to ride a bike—a bike I hadn't actually found yet—around Australia.

There was silence. Westy sat back in his chair and pondered. My heart pounded.

'OK mate, we'll work something out.' That was it.

So, Clare, Craig and Westy—the most important people, who could make or break the plan—were OK with it. Now I really had to do it.

6 THE BIKE THE UNIVERSE LANDED

The search for the bike went on. Whenever I wasn't working or sleeping I was thinking about it. What the right bike might be, how to get it, how to pay for it. Another month rolled by with no result. I turned over and over the problem late at night, a constant chain of repetitive, relentless thoughts without conclusion. With all the bureaucratic negotiations and wrangling, I'd over-complicated things and backed myself into a corner; I just couldn't see a way out of the maze.

And then, in the way that women often do, my wife one day just casually solved the problem that'd had me stumped for months. Yeah, she googled it.

Within five minutes she'd found an article somewhere

in cyberspace from a South Australian newspaper dating back to 2007 about the University of Adelaide winning the Greenfleet Technology class of the World Solar Car Challenge—an annual race from Darwin to Adelaide with vehicles using alternative energy. The University of Adelaide's mechanical engineering team, led by a Dr Colin Kestell, won the Greenfleet class (for fuel-efficient and low-carbon vehicles) on a motorcycle called the Bio Bike. As my eyes scanned ahead on the article, my heart jumped. The winning bike ran on ... used cooking oil.

That's it, I thought. If the University of Adelaide was involved then you could bet the bike was properly registered and insured. I brought up the phone number for the university and called them straightaway.

'May I speak with Dr Kestell, please.' It was only as my call was being put through that I realised I'd never even met an academic before, and I had no idea what I would say to this guy.

The call was picked up and a distinctly English voice said, 'Colin Kestell.' I immediately launched into my introductions, but I could tell he thought I was another of the dozen crackpots that probably rang him up every month with ideas for bio-diesel washing machines and golf carts.

With impeccable manners he politely went about the process of getting me off the phone so he could get on with his day. I left my number with him and hung up, convinced that he thought I was full of shit. Much to my surprise, an hour later he called me back. He said he'd mentioned my call to some of his students who, luckily for me, had read my books. He'd then called my publisher to confirm I was legit. Now he asked me how he could help.

Our conversation was perfect. Colin Kestell was an academic, but he certainly understood guys like me. Within ten minutes we had worked out a plan for getting the university to lend me their Bio Bike in such a way that I could legally ride it right around Australia and do it while properly insured, with no dire consequences to the university if I decided to ride it into a semitrailer or a school bus.

Excited, I then rang Greg Quail to tell him I'd just obtained the use of the only properly road-registered and insured bio-diesel motorcycle in the country. Greg was typically animated; he said he'd film it even without a TV contract.

'What?' I was stunned.

'Fuck it, Pauli, it's too good an idea not to film.'

'What about the cost?'

'Mate, if you can find the sponsorship to do the ride and provide a support truck, then I'll put a cameraman in the truck and cover the cost of all the filming and my guy's expenses.'

That was it. Greg was as good as his word: not only did he enlist the services of a cameraman, he also set up a website to promote my trip (www.thegoodoil.tv).

The next day I called Colin back to arrange a date for me to fly to Adelaide to trial the Bio Bike—which was apparently named 'Betty'.

'How about next month?' said Colin. I could hear him turning pages in his diary.

'Sounds like a plan, Colin.'

Next, I called my lawyer, Mr Digby or 'Diggers'.

I'd always liked the idea of having a lawyer—to help with this kind of thing, mind you, not to get me off because I just stabbed someone with a pitchfork. Diggers came recommended by a couple of friends who swore by his rabid legal mind. If Diggers could deal with *them*—and they *were* the kinds of dudes who might stab someone with a pitchfork—then a guy like me should present no real problems. As usual, he wrapped his head around my situation in one phone call. The contract and all the relevant paperwork was in the mail to the university's lawyer that day.

The next day, I leaned back in my chair, the office air-conditioning whirring quietly in the background. Westy was at lunch and mine was sitting on the desk in front of me looking sad and a little soggy. My computer blinked with an incoming message and I focused on the screen. Colin had just received Diggers' paperwork and had emailed to say there should be no problems at all. Wow. In 24 hours I had landed a bike; now all I needed to do was get over to Adelaide and ride it.

Colin's email included a few photos of Betty the Bio Bike. I sat there holding my sandwich and staring at the bike, imagining the ride. It looked uncomfortable. But something about it felt so right. This trip was about me, a former rig worker, sponsored by oil service companies, riding a bio-diesel-fuelled bike around Australia. At the end of the trip, after I'd recouped my costs, I planned to sell the support truck and give any leftover funds to charity. Everyone wins. Perfect.

I heard the tyres and gearbox of a powerful car clatter over the asphalt and pull up outside. The car's door slammed shut, closely followed by the large voice and banter of one Shaun Southwell. Shaun is the Western Australian manager of a large oilfield supply and fabrication firm we do business with. He's a tall, good-looking, completely confident, swaggering kind of Aussie bloke. I like Shaun; he's only in his mid thirties and has worked his way up from scratch; he knows his job, and you can rely on him. Above all, he's always got a smile on his face and rarely knocks back the opportunity for a laugh. It's as if he's aware that so many men at his stage of their career take themselves too seriously; having some fun in his day is the yeast that fluffs Shaun's mind.

He flopped himself into one of Westy's high-backed tub chairs and demanded a coffee.

'What can I do for you today, Mr Southwell?' I asked. 'Apart from explaining the circle work in the car park to Peter when he gets back.'

Shaun grinned. 'Where is he?' Tipping his head towards Westy's empty chair.

'At lunch with the boys.'

'Ah,' nodded Shaun. 'So he won't be back any time soon then.'

'Dunno, mate.'

His coffee arrived and I watched him study our receptionist's backside over the top of his mug as she walked past my desk.

'Anyway, it's not about what you can do for me, numbnuts.' Looking excited, Shaun dived his hand into his jacket pocket and produced an envelope. 'It's what I can do for you today, mate.' The envelope landed on my deck. From the look on his face I knew this had nothing whatsoever to do with work. He was grinning and making car noises while I opened it up.

I looked up from the ticket inside. 'What's the Clipsal 500?'

Shaun nearly fell off his seat. 'For fuck's sake, Pauli, that's like saying, "What's footy?", you pommy girl.'

Obviously the Clipsal is an important event in the Aussie Man Calendar. I continued to look blank.

'The V8s, mate. In Adelaide. Four days of intense piss-drinking, V8 supercars 'n tits, fuckin man nirvana, you muppet. Westy can't make it this year so you get to go compliments of us, everything paid for.'

'In Adelaide, next week.' I couldn't believe it.

'Yup. If you miss this and want to retain any street

cred with the boys you'll have to be in prison, overseas, clinically insane, or already there waiting.' Shaun leaned back and drank his coffee.

'Well, I'd love to, mate.'

Before Shaun had finished dropping another burn-out in our car park, I was on the phone to Colin. He was as surprised as I was.

The universe was lining up for me. A bike, airfare, hotel, booze, food and V8s 'n tits in 24 hours. Wow, I must have done something right in my last life.

That week went by excruciatingly slowly. The uni sent me the factory manual on Betty's power plant. Basically she was an eight-horsepower irrigation-pump single-stroke diesel engine made by Yanmar in Italy, mounted in the only bike the uni's 2006 mechanical engineering class could get, a now twelve-year-old Cagiva W16, coincidentally also made in Italy. The bike now looked a little odd to say the least, but she was a proven performer.

She had certainly proved her mettle during the World Solar Challenge in 2007. Her vitals were impressive: 2.9 litres per 100 kilometres while emitting only 71 grams per kilometre of carbon dioxide—that's over 75 per cent less emissions than a standard diesel engine. Her average speed was 70 kilometres an hour.

Betty looked good on paper, and in a diesel kind of a way she looked OK in pictures as well, although she had been painted a revolting lime green. I looked forward to meeting her, riding her, and painting her another colour. I was starting to sound like Captain Kirk. But as stupid as it might sound to someone who's not a bike rider, it's important to have a bond between rider and bike.

To a rider the bike is everything. It's an extension of the body, an expression of the last shred of rebelliousness still possible within the confined pigeonhole of suburban reality. But it's not an easy thing, a long motorcycle journey. The long-distance motorcycle rider has to challenge unknown roads in new places where anything can happen. Lots of people told me not to ride alone; I would have liked to do this trip with my mate Erwin, but there was only one bio bike. The two of us used to sit in crappy motel rooms between offshore jobs watching old motorcycle movies—*Easy Rider*, *Stone*, *Mad Max*, *On Any Sunday* and the unmissable *Wild One*. Brando's character Johnny is cheesy 1950s bad boy perfection ('What're you rebelling against, Johnny?' asks a girl. 'Whaddya got?' says Johnny). Ever since Mr Brando pulled on that leather jacket and mumbled his way through Lee Marvin's earwax, I have wanted to do that endless motorcycle journey, and there was no one I'd rather do it with than Erwin. But, as much as he wanted to, I knew Erwin couldn't do the trip with me. Which just left me mumbling Marlon Brando lines all by myself.

Brando was by and large the first mainstream Hollywood star to look really good in his leather jacket, and when he wasn't doing that he was busy looking good walking around in his underwear, and thereby started a trend of looking good in leather jackets and underwear. Brando gave birth to the wife beater as a top to be worn by a sweaty man beyond the parameters of the home, while drinking a Stella, while hurling abuse at Stella in his wife beater. You know what I mean. Postwar America could not get enough of the romance of the motorbike.

I remember older guys in the UK talking about the veritable wars that kicked off between the Mods and the Rockers in Britain through the sixties and seventies. Huge two-wheeled hordes of bikers perpetuated the dark outlaw ethos. How bizarre that a form of transport could be linked so tightly with music, sex and crime—all the bad and all the good. The motorcycle will forever seduce a young rebel's mind. When I think about what made me fall in love with bikes, I think about my joy at watching *Easy Rider* for the first time, *Mad Max*'s evil bikers, Steve McQueen's (or rather Bud Ekins's) jump over that fence. The first time I went to the speedway, I stood so close to the track that oil and mud splattered my trackside face on the first turn. My first bike was a second-hand Honda C90. I was fifteen and spotty. Twenty-six years and several bikes later, I still can't get enough.

I've had years of only really being at peace when I'm sitting on a motorcycle with nothing but time to kill. For my ride around Australia I could have had any bike on the Aussie market. But Betty was going to be my ride; she would be the one. An experimental bike, built on a shoestring budget, by students. I knew this was going to pan out, there was just too much synchronicity about it: there was no way I could be a BMW tourist now. No, this ride was going to be about me and Betty.

7 BETTY

The flight to Adelaide was about to board. I got there just in time, the last in as the crew shut the door.

My window seat near the back was the only empty seat on the entire aircraft. It looked impossibly hard to fit into from the aisle. The guy in the aisle seat got up to let me do the sideways shimmy thing, breathing in. It's an interesting challenge to try to get into an economy class window seat without touching the headrest of your seat or the seat in front of you. Either I've grown or economy has shrunk in the last ten years.

I parked my arse, did up the buckle, looked out the window and contemplated how long I had to sit there. Only a few years ago I had been a real air traveller from one job to the next, racking up huge distances all over the world. It took many years to get my platinum frequent-flyer card. By that time I was only flying business class. Then I stopped working on the rigs, and before I knew it, bam, I was demoted. Just a few months earlier I'd finally got a crappy entry-level green card, back to where I'd started over twenty years earlier, and back in economy.

The realisation that I could no longer afford to be an airline snob came crashing down as I leaned forward to scan the contents of the seat pocket and discovered that the seat in front of me could recline into my face. The guy sitting beside me gave a sympathetic nod. 'Just as well it's not a long-haul flight.' He smiled, and stuck out his hand. 'Stephen,' he introduced himself.

'Paul.' I shook his hand, or rather jutted my palm out from my armpit and waved it up and down. We looked like two grown men attempting an impromptu impression of two tyrannosaurus rex thumb wrestling.

It turned out he knew of my books. 'What brings you to Adelaide?' he asked.

'Well, it's research.' I explained my plans, and his smile broadened.

'Well, I'm the Deputy Lord Mayor of Adelaide. I know the university well. How can I help?'

At the end of the flight, I stepped off the plane with Stephen telling me the lord mayor would probably be happy to wave me off at the start of my trip. This promised coverage on the local news, which would be great for my sponsors. Again the universe was surprising me.

I checked into the hotel, left my bags with the concierge and crossed the road. There in front of me was the University of Adelaide. I walked slowly through the campus grounds. The place was a joy to take in. Wonderful old buildings mixed well with their younger, more modern counterparts, generously spaced out with manicured tree-lined pathways. Bespectacled students hurried past me clutching folders and looking worried but intelligent. I called Colin on my mobile, and he directed me to his office.

A small group of students was standing in the doorway when I got there. As I approached they dispersed, filtering past me and out the door. Colin was standing in the middle of his office—which was exactly as I'd imagined it would look. Opposite the door was a large desk facing a window with masses of paper stacked on every surface; a coffee machine and a keyboard could barely be seen under all the books and paper. Across from the bookshelves on the left was an old well-used couch. A large whiteboard hung on the wall covered in technical drawings that looked to me like a map of the London Underground.

'Paul, welcome, I'm Colin Kestell.' Unlike his office, Colin did not look anything like I'd imagined. He was of medium height and build, looked younger than his years and was wonderfully frank in his conversation, spoken in that London accent. He was a lad at heart, one of the boys; I was instantly at ease.

Over the next few hours we went over my plan, then he suddenly stood up and said, 'Look, all this is just academic.' (I couldn't help smiling.) 'You need to ride the bike. Follow me,' he said.

On the way to see Betty, Colin took me on a brief tour of the mechanical engineering building. They had a vast array of resources, from full CAD design level to fabrication. If they'd wanted to, they could have built a bus from scratch, or a Transformer, or both.

I wish I'd had the chance to go to university when I was young, but that opportunity never presented itself. Where I came from, going to uni was not really an option; anyone who wasn't doing serious time or addicted to heroin was considered a high achiever.

We entered a large open-plan workshop full of milling machines, lathes, all manner of welding, drilling and cutting gear immaculately presented for the keen young student to play around with. Colin stopped by the open doors of a small window-lined room and stretched out his arm as if to make a formal introduction. 'There she is, Betty the Bio Bike.'

I walked into the room and stopped to look at her from a distance. She was bigger than I imagined.

'We had her stored in the basement,' Colin said. 'I asked the workshop guys to bring her out and prep her for you.'

I approached her the way cats do a new home. Then, circling her frame, I started firing questions at Colin.

Soon I was on all fours poking my fingers inside the frame, and in less than a minute I was lying flat on my back looking at the drive system. The engine was bolted directly to the modified frame, which had to be widened to take the extra width of the heavy diesel single. There was no gearbox; to comply with the tight fabrication budget the students who built her three years earlier had opted for a Comet 500 series CVT (constant variable transmission) drive system instead of an expensive gearbox. The drive is transferred from the engine shaft by a spring-loaded round cup that extends towards the bike, squashing a rubber drive V-belt. The more you open up the throttle the faster the cup spins; the faster the cup spins the more the rubber drive belt is squashed; the squashing of the rubber belt expands it open, stretching it to the outer diameter of the spinning cup and thereby rotating it much faster. The rubber belt is connected in turn to the drive sprocket via a custom-made idler shaft system and from there via a conventional chain to the sprocket on the rear wheel.

Much like a golf cart or many modern scooter drive systems, Betty was simply twist and go; she looked like the easiest bike in the world to ride. Colin explained to me that the bio-fuel is corrosive and over time eats the fuel lines, so these were made from a very heavy-duty hose. She had a custom-made fairing and instrument cluster displaying speed on an old-school cable-driven analogue gauge that also contained an old rolling mechanical odometer, engine RPM, oil temp and battery voltage. Everything else on the bike was as per the original 1997 Cagiva W16.

The bike had been donated to the uni, as was the L100AE-DE Yanmar industrial engine—Japanese design but Italian built. It's an extremely common engine, found on irrigation pumps or in boats. Finding parts would be easy, as would troubleshooting on the side of the road. In terms of consumables everything was off-the-shelf gear available from major suppliers. She was running Pirelli MT90 tires, again Italian, 21-inch on the front and seventeen-inch on the rear.

Next I met Rob, Steve and Phil who worked in the uni's workshop—great guys. What a fantastic place this must be to study; I envied the students the opportunity to learn from people like Colin and men with real industry experience like the workshop guys. I thought teaching must be very rewarding, too. Colin was completely devoted to his craft, and after meeting some of his students I could see that they were im-passioned by his method. 'His lectures aren't boring,' one student told me. I heard later that Colin once walked into his class dressed as a gorilla.

Colin had a helmet, jacket and gloves ready for me, and we rolled Betty out of the workshop. 'Off you go,' he said. 'Take it for a good run, Paul.'

I slotted the key into the ignition and turned it: the little red glow light came on; I hit the start button, and her starter motor sprang to life, the single piston pumping, her big round steel impeller spinning beneath its cover. As I twisted the throttle to get more fuel through the injectors I had to pull on the front brake to stop from lurching forward. Then it hit me, the most amazing aroma of cooking oil. It was an unmistakable food smell, a combination of fish 'n' chips and greasy fry-up. I turned in the saddle and looked down at the light grey smoke puffing in time with the engine's KA DONK, KA DONK, KA DONK.

I took Betty out of the university grounds and we cautiously circled the block, before exploring further afield. Her riding position was very upright. The foot pegs were low, and directly under my knees, like riding on a Vespa. Sitting there with my legs at a strange angle, I felt as if I were sitting in an office in a typing pool, rather than on a fairly big Enduro bike. Betty's handling characteristics were like nothing I'd felt before, but then again this bike was one of a kind. Her 160 kilos fell into corners halfway round on the right side, responding to minimal handlebar pressure more than any weight transfer. I assumed this was due to the big heavy impeller spinning at her centre of gravity. The opposite effect on the left had me hanging over and pulling her round. It wasn't until I got onto a highway that I really started to worry: the vibration through the entire front end was massive, like holding onto a jackhammer. But having said all that, she worked, and worked well. Her top speed was 70 kph, not too bad considering that on this first ride I travelled 100 kilometres on just 2.9 litres of used cooking oil and waste animal fats.

I pulled back into the university grounds that afternoon feeling both euphoric and more than a little worried. I was hopelessly out of my depth; even the janitor in that place had a better knowledge base on this stuff than me. Plus, Betty was only designed to get from Darwin to Adelaide. Now I was going to push the envelope and attempt to take her all the way round the continent. I knew it was a long shot, but what else was I going to do: fly home, forget the whole thing and mow the lawn? No way, this was a challenge.

There was no real choice for me anyway. This motorcycle worked, it was registered and insured, and most importantly, it was free.

I didn't need to be at the Clipsal until the following morning, so I suggested we go and have a celebratory drink. 'Sounds great,' said Colin. One of Colin's students, Kelly, came with us, as we wandered into the city. After a few drinks, Kelly had to leave; I grabbed a single malt and sat down, keen to talk more about Betty with Dr Kestell.

He was direct. 'Mate, Betty's a good bike. The kids who put her together got the right learning curve constructing her, the race they won from Darwin to Adelaide was just icing really. She was never intended to cover that kind of distance.' I sat back and said nothing.

'Look, from what you've told me, she's the only bike available. With enough spare parts you could make it.'

He flipped over a coaster and pulled a pen from his top pocket. I shifted around to see what he was doing. *Total distance, roughly*, he scribbled. 'Average speed, right, that's less than half the working life of the engine.' I smiled. 'Just keep the oil topped up, order enough drive belts, sprockets and filters, and the rest is easy to get. We can even give you a spare engine and CVT drive.'

'What about the vibration?' I asked, and he shrugged.

'That engine is bolted to the frame, there's no quick cheap fix for that. You might want to think about changing the seat too, mate, there's no quick cheap fix for your arse either. Good luck to ya, cheers.'

This is possibly the silliest thing I've ever tried to do, I thought.

During the course of our conversation, I found out that Colin used to work for British Aerospace. 'What did you do there?' I was fascinated.

'I was on the team that designed the Exocet Missile System,' he said. Even I had heard of that. 'And the Martin-Baker Ejection Seat.'

I couldn't believe it. 'My father used one of them,' I said, and we sat there talking late into the night, the bar emptying out around us; only a few punters parked on stools bar-side sat nursing beers and what looked like troubled lives.

It turned out that Colin was far too interested in bikes to stop at Betty. 'Well, we're in the process of designing a bike to break the bio-fuel land speed record.'

I sat forward; the hairs on my arm stood up. That would *definitely* be the silliest thing I've ever tried to do. 'That's getting a bit serious, mate,' I said.

He smiled. 'Well, every aspect of it will be overseen by myself, and it's a great experience for the students—they get right into it.'

'Who's riding it?' I asked.

He could see the look in my eye. 'Well, no one yet.'

'You're in charge.'

He sipped his whisky. 'Mmm.' He nodded.

'And you used to be a rocket scientist,' I said.

'Well, I suppose you could put it that way.'

He knew what I was going to say way before I said it.

'I want to do it,' I said.

He finished his drink and eyeballed me through the bottom of his glass. I sat up straighter, and tried to look like a man responsible enough not to crash a bloody fast experimental bio-fuelled bike in a land speed record attempt. He leaned across the table and shook my hand.

8 GETTING TO KNOW YOU

The Clipsal 500 hit me the next morning. Southwell was wound up like a kid in a toy shop. He led me up into a private stand trackside, handed me a cold beer and beamed. 'You're gonna fuckin love this, mate.'

By the end of the first day I was happily pissed. I was also surprised at the sheer number of really hammered middle-aged guys I saw staggering about with empty beer cartons on their heads. One guy had a huge Holden flag tied around his neck; running flat out in his underpants across an open stretch of grass and yelling wildly his cape flapping behind him, he looked like a semi-naked overweight superhero. He was closely followed by 'Ford Man', also in a cape and underpants.

Shaun was in his element. We looked at the strippers,

drank too much, put on silly hats, smoked cigars, and talked about cars, bikes, tits 'n shit. Clipsal might as well be called Man World.

'You know they limited everyone at Bathurst to one carton per day this year,' he leaned in to yell at me over the roar of the cars, spit hitting my inner ear. 'Heaps of blokes snuck in at night and buried cartons all over the place, then the next day there were hundreds of piss-heads wandering about with those collapsible shovels looking for their beer.'

I looked at him. 'That was you, wasn't it, mate?'

One day at the races was enough for me, though; the next day I was at the uni again, this time with my head in the High Performance Diesel Motorcycle (HPDM) project. At this stage it was physically nothing more than a car engine and a rear swing arm sitting on a big table, but the plans were impressive. The wiring harness alone spilling out of the engine was intimidating, like rainbow-coloured spaghetti hanging out in every direction. Each individual wire would have to be dealt with in order to get that engine started. I heard later that after weeks of testing, the students finally got it going by wiring up the cigarette lighter.

On my last night in Adelaide, Shaun and I sat down in a great little restaurant and actually had an intelligent, mature conversation. I was as surprised by this as he was. He was extremely supportive of my plans for Betty, as mad as it must have sounded to him. It was good to sit there and talk about our lives and futures; I saw a side of him that I suspect few people do.

The next day Colin saw me off back to Perth. We had made a plan for me to return in two weeks so I could spend a few days with Rob and Steve in the workshop getting familiar with Betty: practising changing out filters, lines, sprockets, injectors, blown tyres, chains, the idler shaft setup and the CVT drive—basically everything. I already had an extensive list of parts and consumables as well as complete detailed manuals for the bike engine—both would be put to good use after my next trip to Adelaide as Betty would then be freighted to Perth so I could get down to the business of pulling her to pieces and putting her back together again. I could practise changing out the entire engine if need be. For the first time since this idea raised its head and poked me in the eye, I was confident I could make it happen. I'd then put her in the back of the support truck, along with the spare parts, and drive from Perth to Adelaide, from where I'd start my journey the next day.

The two weeks dragged while I waited to return to Adelaide. On my first day back in the office I tried to remain focused on my job, and resisted the urge to jump on the phone and start organising; I couldn't wait to start planning. I came home from work to find that Clare, bless her, had gone to a specialty map store in the city and come home with an excellent, detailed map book of Australia as well as a giant fold-out map.

After supper I disappeared into the garage, opened up the fold-out map and lay on the floor looking at it. I had a rough idea of the route I wanted to take, but now I started to mark it out and break it up into various stages. I reckoned there would be seven in all, so I would need seven different support drivers, as no one person could take three months off work to accompany me. I listed some names in the corner of the map, opened a beer and picked up the phone. Now was as good a time as any to enlist my helpers. Six of the guys were old mates from the rigs, and then there was my father-in-law, Phil—he had to be there. We hadn't spent much time together other than the odd weekend visit, but I'd been sleeping with his daughter for the last seven years—it was about time I got to know the guy.

By the early hours of the morning I'd almost worked through my list. Waking guys up got me a great response: 'Do you know what fuckin time it is, Pauli?' But once they'd calmed down, they quickly got interested. There was a lot of laughter, a lot of 'You're gonna *what*?', but without fail they said yes.

Now, yes was good, yes works, but when it comes to guys who work in the oilfield, yes means shit. Not because the guy who says yes doesn't mean it, it's just that in the oilfield shit happens. In the last ten years I was working offshore I said yes to everything— weddings, Christmases, birthdays, funerals, armed hold-ups—but didn't actually make it to any of them. So the yes from the six who work in oil was taken with a bucket of salt.

Still, I was so grateful for their enthusiam; I would think that most people would consider themselves lucky if they could count on one hand the people that would do shit like this with them. During the course of my life I have managed to hold on to a small community of friends that will not only do this kind of shit with me, but often; without knowing it, again and again these guys save the day.

My support truck driver for the first stage—from Adelaide to Melbourne—was a bloke called Howard Fletcher who I met in Brunei back in 1995. He was now based in Brisbane, still in drilling but deskbound. Howard and I are the same age, same height, same build, and we've both got the same mad-keen motorcycle thing going on, but that's where the similarities end. Howard is quiet, calm, and doesn't fly off the handle like I do. He's also sound with mechanics and has bags of experience driving trucks, which is why I wanted to line him up first.

Second stage, Melbourne to Sydney, was supposed to be Neil Boath, a rig manager and rider, a typical hardcore drilling hand. I met him on a jack up in Bangladesh and we've been mates ever since. He said yes, but before the month was up Neil was sent to the Middle East and Shane Edwards stepped in. Shane is 40 years old and fitter than I was at twenty, another crazy rider. Shane's not oilfield, he doesn't take drugs, smoke, swear much, or fart in public, but he is one of the funniest blokes I've ever been drunk with. He's also one of those super-capable guys who can fix anything or anyone; he's generous to a fault and never late for anything. Most weekends Clare and I have breakfast with Shane and his wife Katrina, who's in possession of the most distracting cleavage in Western Australia. Her sense of humour often makes coffee come out my nose. Another friend at these breakfasts is Jools, who runs a funeral home, always looks amazing, spoils my daughter, and always has a story to tell. She's the woman you want to deal with you when you die; the thought of getting burned or embalmed by her sits well with me. I've always had a Sophia Loren fantasy that involved a bit of cooking and pain; it's just a shame that when it does finally happen, I'll be dead.

My father-in-law, Filthy Phil as I call him, was on board for stage three. He was only too happy to drive for me, which was great. I've got to set the record straight, though: Phil is only known as Filthy because every time I go over to visit him in Sydney he's in the back shed with his head in an engine and grease up to his ears. Filthy's shed is bigger than their house and goes beyond the realms of any man's world-shed scenario. It's a real working man's shed, with a classic vintage Plymouth project and enough spare parts, tools, and bits of man stuff to make Steptoe himself develop a man crush. He's even got his own forklift. Filthy is a talented man:

he works as a panel beater, truck driver, mechanic and rebuilder of all things with wheels and engines. He knows the roads like the back of his filthy hand. He would get me from Sydney to Brisbane, no worries.

There's a driller who appears in my first book, a young, well-built maniac of a Scotsman by the name of Donald. Everyone else calls him Alistair. After sixteen years of knowing him, I still don't quite know why I call him Donald, though I really should know considering he's one of my closest mates. Once on an offshore drilling rig Donald was having a bad day on the drill floor and in a memorable moment picked up the tool pusher and attempted to throw him over the side and into the South China Sea. We managed to stop him, and that was the last time I stood next to Donald on a drill floor.

We had however remained close over the years, in an oilfield kind of a way, and by that I mean he'd be on a rig in Norway and I'd be on a rig in Africa and never did the twain meet, unless they happened to crew change from different sides of the planet through the same airport on the same day at the same time in the same departure lounge. Yes, you'd be surprised how often that happened. And once we'd rebooked our flights after missing our connections, sobered up and paid for any damages, we would go back to our different corners of the world until the next time the universe wanted a laugh. Much to my amazement, the last time we bumped into each other was one year ago right here in Perth, the most isolated city on the planet. I walked out of a lunch meeting at a Japanese restaurant with Westy, full of sake and with no memory of the business we'd sorted out in the first five minutes, and bumped straight into Donald. He had just arrived in town, and was working as a rig manager of a new build jack-up drilling in the northwest of the state. I was so happy to see his face, right there where I lived, and not in a blank airport in some shit hole. I knew that if there was anyone who would be fun to hit the road with, it would be Donald.

When I called him he said yes, and to his credit he did everything he could to get the time off. But through a chain of events that was beyond Donald's control, while I was on the road he had to push the button a man in his position never wants to push. The rig was evacuated as the well lost control and a sub-sea blowout crippled his operation.

My brother-in-law jumped in at the last minute to drive for Donald on stage four, Brisbane to Darwin. I've already told you about Clare's older brother Mathew—musician, band manager, music lover and filmmaker. He's not at all what you're thinking: he's much, much worse. That's all I'm going to say about Matt for now.

Stage five—Darwin to Broome—Gavin Kelly. 'Fuckin Pauli, it's a bit fuckin late, mate.' He coughed for a full minute; Gav could smoke for Scotland. 'You better be on fuckin fire or some shit, mate, eh. What's gan on?' I ran my spiel past him, asked him the question. There was a pause. 'You want me te fuckin what?' I repeated my request, and there was another pause. 'Eh, what fuckin truck?' I told him again. 'Aye, OK, ne bother, mate. Hey I've got a fuckin truck licence as well, man.' I was happy. Even though he works in oil and is away a lot, if Gavin said yes, I just knew he was going to be there.

Southwell was a yes for stage six, Broome to Perth, but had to pull out because of—you guessed it—the oilfield. Again Clare's family jumped in to help; this time it was Clare's younger sister, Carrie, who's in the navy. She's a physical training instructor—still very much a lady but hard as fuck, and not what you're thinking— much, much better.

Last but not least was my old mate, Erwin Herczeg. I wanted him for stage seven, Perth back to Adelaide. Of course he said yes. Erwin's a company man now, a drilling manager; of course he was still offshore when his turn came.

By daybreak, the seven stages were marked out on the map, complete with dates, distances, places to overnight and get the truck serviced, and each of my seven support drivers. With Oswald making the odd visit, I had been in the garage all night, and now the morning sun cracked through the gaps between the door and the floor. I had worked it all out, or as much as I could.

I stood up, stretched, and drank a mouthful of cold coffee. I had to be at the office in two hours.

Clare came down the stairs carrying Lola and looking bemused. 'All night, honey, you need to rest.' She set Lola down and walked around the mess of paper and maps on the floor, my scribbles on everything; she could see I'd had some kind of breakthrough.

It had already been decided that Clare and Lola would come with me on the next trip to Adelaide as I wanted them to see what I had been doing. I'm truly blessed, my Clare is supportive and infinitely patient with me. I also love how she doesn't skirt around the edges of anything, she just dives right in. I often ask myself how I got so lucky.

'So we're going to Adelaide so you can practise on the bike,' she said now.

'Yup, the boys will walk me through everything, and I'll also get a good look at the HPDM project.'

She looked thoughtful. 'That's the speed bike for the salt flats, right baby? I don't like the speed project, it's too dangerous.' She looked over at Lola, who was busy fitting her dummy into the cat's ear.

'That bike is nothing like Betty,' I reassured her. 'It's very well engineered. I trust Colin, he's not going to hand over a machine that's not up to the task. Don't worry, everything will work out fine.' That's what I thought she needed to hear.

'I don't like it: you don't have any salt-flat riding

experience and that bike is experimental.' She had that look in her eye.

'Look baby, it's going to be perfectly organised and as safe as we can make it.'

Safer than what? I thought privately. Putting on roller skates and strapping an Acme rocket to my back? Which reminded me, after our trip I had to fly from Adelaide to Sydney to sit down with Diggers and draft a will that would cover all scenarios.

Fortunately, Clare switched her attention back to my other crazy project. 'So you'll be going with the bike from here to Adelaide once you're ready?' She sat down on a box of oil filters.

I nodded. 'That's right.'

Lola, having successfully inserted her dummy into the cat's mouth, now picked up an axle bolt and stared beadily at poor Oswald's anus.

'Can we come with you in the truck instead of flying to Adelaide?'

I was pumped. 'That would be great, honey—are you sure?'

She laughed. 'Yeah, it'll be fun, our first family roadie.'

At that point Oswald let out a howl and then shot past us, Lola with the axle bolt in pursuit.

9 THERE IS NO PLAN B

The flight to Adelaide was soon upon us. Clare loves the place, and spent the two days we were there exploring with Lola. I liked Adelaide too. I could live there, even if for no other reason than it's closer to Sydney than Perth.

If I add up all the years on the rigs, I've spent two-thirds of my life somewhere else other than Australia. Staying in one place is a treat for me now, because for too many years I was just another expatriate, living in a country that wasn't mine. Living in the oilfield means living on the no-man's land of the rig and moving to a new country with every job. It does broaden the mind and your perception of life, and it puts a great deal into perspective. But after the crew has scattered it can leave you feeling alone and a little out of place at the ten-year oilfield family Christmas dinner.

Wherever I was, I would miss home, perhaps because of the way the oilfield and some cities just hem you in. I miss the open spaces and rich colour of Australia, and the vastness that you know is only a two-hour drive away if you need it. That empty space is there, it's big enough to swallow up all of Europe. That longing to be home would come into my mind and run on the hamster wheel for hours, I think because I spent so much of my life in the boxed-up world of life on a rig, where space is a valuable commodity.

In Adelaide, while Clare and Lola were sightseeing, I was back at the university. I was happy with the preparations for the ride. Thanks to Rob from the workshop, I had fuel filters, CVT drive belts, and a new battery.

Steve then walked me through his fabrication process on the HPDM. The bike was going to be a monster. Its frame weight was 75 kilos, the wheel base was 2.4 metres, with a Holden Astra turbo diesel engine plumbed into a Harley Dyna gearbox. The frame was—in a word—perfect; the engine sat balanced with only a few millimetres of clearance. I had already joined the DLRA—the Dry Lakes Racing Association. 'You're going to need proper leathers for the salt, mate.' Steve smiled.

The DLRA scrutineers would have to make several trips to the uni, making sure the bike conformed to their rule book. The plan was that the bike would go to

Speed Week in March 2011 and start speed trials at Lake Gairdner, South Australia.

I was captivated by the amount of enthusiasm and skill behind this motorcycle. The students were as fascinating to talk to as the staff. They sat me down in a huge room filled with computers and showed me the computational fluid dynamics software that produced the fairing design. I couldn't wait to ride this thing one day.

Colin and I talked through the HPDM project, his office coffee helping my brain to keep pace with his stream of motorcycle consciousness. We slowly worked out a plan for our week on the salt in two years. Then he took me back to see the engine running on a dyno test setup operated by his students. The engine looked strange mounted in a steel jig in the test room. We were all wearing industrial hearing protection, staring at it from behind glass. 'Increase rpm, more air.' One of Colin's students sat in front of a bank of computers turning dials, his eyes darting from one screen to another. 'Max power,' he said. The engine was screaming in its frame. Their calculations—encompassing the distance I had to get up to speed before the speed trap in the flying kilometre, versus the bike's weight, drag, max power, acceleration, gearing—had me getting to 260 kilometres per hour at best, not enough to beat the American who currently held the land-speed record for a bio-diesel motorcycle at 267 kph. I thought about going on a diet.

The class was unfazed by this, however; everyone simply focused on working through the problem, charging into conversations I couldn't keep up with, so I nodded and smiled, fiddled with the change in my pocket and ended up thinking about naked cheerleaders cavorting in jello with a giant beach ball.

Whatever the outcome would be, I was just happy to get the opportunity to spend time with the students and guys like Colin and the fellas in the workshop, especially Rob. He was a fountain of knowledge and couldn't do enough to help me with my preparations to ride Betty. On our last night we all had a beer together. The spares were boxed up and Betty was ready for her freight trip over to me in Perth. 'See you in a month,' I called as the cab pulled away that night.

From Adelaide, we flew to Sydney, where Clare and Lola caught up with her family and I went to see my lawyer to draft my will.

Diggers' office was comfortable. Soft light from the warm sunset spread an orange glow over his bookshelves; I could smell the sea. He gathered up some paperwork and offered me a drink. 'Just a coffee, thanks mate,' I said.

'I'll be right back,' he said.

I had my eyes closed for a moment, tired from the week's running around; a wind chime nearby made my lids heavier. When he came back in, the smell of fresh coffee filled the air. He sat down, crossed his legs and regarded me. 'Let's begin. I'm going to ask you some direct questions, Paul. I want honest, direct answers, is that OK?'

The process took a few gruelling hours. His manner was relaxed but you could tell the wheels were turning. Designing a will is important for everyone, and I didn't find any of it confronting, but it raised my buried worries about the element of risk in what I was planning to do. What if something *did* happen? I thought about the risks I was taking in riding Betty and leaving my girls alone for three months. I thought about the danger of the speed trials, the possibility of serious injury or death. The shadows in Diggers' office filled up with doubt.

I rubbed my eyes. 'I'll take that drink, mate, if you don't mind.'

'Not at all,' he said, and poured me a whisky. 'We're almost finished.' He went over the paperwork between the university and me, then closed his file and sat back. 'You're all set. If something goes wrong now, is there a plan B?'

I laughed. 'No mate, it's plan A or back to work.'

'Right. Well, good luck and be careful.' Diggers raised his mug.

'Cheers, mate.' I finished my drink.

'Don't mention it.'

He had brought up every possible scenario and we'd talked each one through. I was at ease now. I knew that no matter what, my girls would be OK.

The next morning I had a few hours to myself, so I jumped on a bus and headed off to my mate Dare's motorcycle shop. Well, shop is not the right word; 'complete mecca for bike enthusiasts' would be more appropriate.

It'd been about five years since Dare went into partnership with his mate Rod and opened Deus Ex Machina (God From The Machine), two storeys of homage to all things motorcycle. I remember the day he first acquired the building, formerly a furniture store covering a whole corner block of Sydney's busy Parramatta Road. Dare had also just purchased what would be the shop's main countertop—an entire intact ten-pin bowling alley lane. It weighed a ton; a huge group of us staggered across Parramatta Road with this gigantic wooden thing, and getting it through the front door was a nightmare. But now it looks fantastic, sitting proudly in the middle of the shop.

Between them Dare and Rod have carved out a nice niche in the bike world. Whenever I visit I always end up spending the whole day there. After a few years they opened an excellent instore café, so now you don't even have to leave for lunch. One half of the main shop sells clothing; they've also got an extensive bookshop, and as far as the bikes go, well, they sell stock machines, full custom builds, classic bikes and bicycles as well. Like

I said, it's heaven on a stick for motorbike fanatics like me.

Sooner or later, I always end up in the workshop. The man then running the show was another mate of mine, Matt Bromley. He was a Perth boy, a doting father and a complete genius in front of a motorcycle. I've learned a lot from Matty; he's patient and methodical, his machines are perfect in every way.

This was a typically busy midweek day in Deus. I wandered in and ran straight into Dare and Ben, the store manager. We had coffee while I ran through my plans for the trip. They both jumped in with their usual enthusiasm for anything a bit different.

'When you pass through Sydney, make sure you stop by. Matt will service the bike and Taka can organise any spares you need,' said Ben, smiling.

'Why don't you have a chat to Taka and Matt now?' added Dare. His relaxed aura is palpable. When Dare's not messing about on bikes he's all about surfing, and he's got that surfer's calm about him. He reminds me of Erwin; they both have that vibe of appearing to be completely relaxed and yet capable of anything at the same time.

Following their suggestion, I made my way over to see Taka. Taka is Deus's one-man parts encyclopedia. A Japanese national who made Sydney his home some years back, his English is faultless and his brain box goes at a million miles an hour. As soon as I started telling him about Betty he knew exactly what I was on about, and asked to look at my spares list. He pointed out several items I hadn't thought of and was off like a shot to order them for me.

Matty Bromley was exactly where I expected to find him, out the back with his head in a frame and a coffee perched on his workbench. He was full of good advice as well. I was very grateful to know if I did have any problems during the trip I could count on help from the Deus guys. Matt asked about Betty's fuel and air filters; we talked about the oil, the tyres, and he gave me the number of a guy who sells these amazing air cushion seats. 'Mate, you're going to need to get one of these seats, that Cagiva will shred your arse before you get as far as Sydney.' He paused and placed the end of the ratchet he was holding against his chin. 'What's the vibration like?'

I laughed. 'Horrible.'

'Hmmmm.' He walked back to his workbench, past the other mechanics zoned into their work. 'I could go to town on it, mate, but it's going to take some time; what's your budget like?'

I knew I didn't have the time or the funds to get the bike over to Matty to play with before I set out, and I also knew he'd end up building a whole new bike once he started. 'Nah mate, can't do it.'

'Well, no worries, Pauli, we'll look after you when you come through.'

I told him about the website Quail TV had set up, and we tapped into the web; Matt laughed when he saw the picture of Betty on the laptop screen, then leaned in to get a look at her engine. 'Jesus, Pauli, you're keen, mate. Is this some sort of payback for all those years on the rigs or what?' I smiled. 'What's the top end power like, lots of torque from that diesel?'

'It sits on 70 at 3000 rpm on a flat road.'

He was deep in thought. 'How many teeth on the drive sprocket?'

'Forty-four,' I said.

'OK, we'll order you a 39-tooth rear sprocket—it'll be here in an hour or so. Take it back to Perth and see if it gives you more speed.' He explained that if we changed down a tooth on the drive sprocket the CVT drive might start to slip, but five teeth down on the rear drive sprocket should give me perhaps ten kilometres per hour more speed. We had some lunch and talked bikes, babies (he's a new father too) and the HPDM project. I asked Matty if he was up for a trip to the salt to have a go on the speed bike. 'Mate, I'm in,' he said. 'They're all nutters at Speed Week.'

We shook hands and I jumped in another cab to the airport, sprocket in hand, feeling good about everything. I'd put some fears to rest, faced down some internal dragons, been warmed by the generosity of old friends, and even better, had possibly gained another ten kph.

10 PPPPP

A wise man once said: Proper Planning Prevents Piss Poor Performance.

Two weeks after we got back from Sydney, Betty turned up at my house. I wheeled her off the back of a truck and into the middle of my garage. She sat there surrounded by motorcycles and shelves of bike gear. I prepared to disassemble her, and Clare's car was relegated to the driveway. Each night after work was wholly devoted to this, while my weekends were spent drafting letters to potential sponsors. During the two weeks I'd been waiting for Betty to arrive I'd written reams of emails and letters.

Right at the beginning of the worst global financial crisis since the Second World War, I was running around asking the oil industry for money. Yeah, I know, excellent timing. Our government was about to start handing out free money, calling it a 'stimulus package'. I lay on the garage floor under the bike and listened to late night radio, stunned. When not on the drill floor, I've lived in this marvellous country for the last 25 years. Whether here or overseas Australians are doers, we get things done, we can deal with anything. Why was the Rudd government giving a nation famous for its adaptability and hardiness a giant cash dummy?

I'm not qualified to ramble on, but I also couldn't believe the power brokers who head up the world's banking systems had let it get to this. My cat could offer better guidance on the merits of lending money to people you know cannot repay it, but these people— who, I assume, hold MBAs, earn seven-figure salaries, and have a corner office—thought it was a great idea. We were all going to pay for it, one way or another, further down the line. But this particular financial pandemic was causing me problems right here and now. Suddenly, no one was interested in backing me. I thought about selling one of my bikes to help pay for the project, and my publisher offered to give me an advance on future book sales, but I was reluctant to go down those paths. I was despondent. All I had was an idea and the bike.

To do this trip I'd worked out I needed to raise $100,000. I had to find a support truck and rig it out with a cage, ramp, wheel brace, shelves, two 400-litre custom baffled fuel cells with proper electric fuel pumps, separate power, cover it with a good tarp, then get appropriate signs on it. Add to that bike-repair tools, a mountain of spares for Betty, including a spare donor bike, communications gear, insurance, accommodation, flights, food—the list went on and on.

Then to my complete surprise, during the week I spent in my garage pulling the bike apart each night, I landed seven sponsors totalling $85,000. The oil community in Western Australia got behind me—not the big players, but the smaller firms. I was amazed and humbled, especially since I knew giving that much was a big deal to them. To a big multi-national that's not a great deal of money—their budget for paperclips would be bigger than that. But to these small service companies and third party firms it was a significant outlay.

Still, it was going to be tight; everything would be second-hand but it had to look decent. The donor bike was the hardest thing to find. Cagiva sold very few W16 Enduro bikes in Australia twelve years ago. Eventually I started looking overseas but had no luck. In desperation, I wrote to Cagiva asking for the landed cost of a frame, front forks, triple clamp, bars, controls, levers, swing arm, wheels, tank, seat and a partridge in a Cagiva tree; the sum they quoted me was horrendous.

I gave up and started looking for a truck, all the while organising agreement letters, accommodation bookings, flights, ordering spare parts plus patches for my jacket and stickers for the truck and bike with all the sponsors' brands in the right size and format, and managing negotiations between my publisher and the production company. As well, late into the night I tinkered on Betty until she was completely disassembled. On occasion Lola helped by picking up a nut or bolt and eating it.

A support truck was proving tricky to find too; it had to be a dual cab to accommodate the driver, the cameraman and the large amount of filming gear he'd need to access from the cab. It also had to be over three tonnes but registered to drive on a car licence because only two of my seven support drivers had a truck licence. All in all, my requirements meant finding the right truck was as likely as finding a clean signed pair of Jeremy Clarkson's favourite driving panties in the specials bin at Coles.

But I couldn't let it bog me down, I couldn't stop, because the minute I did it would all look too hard, especially with a full-time job, and a wife and child to spend time with. During this period, there was no time for anything other than work, family, trip. I missed everything else, especially sleep. My garage looked like someone had set off a bomb in a bike parts warehouse.

Lola was now eighteen months old, and already displaying character traits that I found so familiar. Her new doll, a present from her aunty Jools, was abandoned in the corner; she was more interested in how fast her pram would go. Lola would often join me in the garage, handing me spanners and bashing things while chattering to me. None of it made real sense yet, but it was her sweet voice and interest in what I was doing that cracked me up. 'Daddy, Nemo, Wiggles, Dada, HEY, BIKE DADA BIKE, no, no cheeky . . .' BANG, BANG, BANG. I'd look around and she'd be swinging a wrench down onto her mother's new car. As soon as I turned around again she'd be off, her legs a blur as she races down the hall waving my wrench over her head. I'd come back later to discover sultanas, crayons and a dummy shoved up the car exhaust. I know she has my temper, but I hope as the years go by she also has my internal early-warning system and bullshit detector. I hope she takes life by the balls, and any boys that come around too.

Right when I needed it the most, it happened again: in one week I found both the perfect truck and a pristine Cagiva W16 garaged since new with only 3000 k's on the clock. Even better, both were in Australia and both were available for the right price. The truck was ex-council, downgraded and registered to drive on a car licence, four-tonne capacity, dual cab, with a nice flat tray. I picked up the bike for half the cost of the spares quote from Cagiva. It arrived, again on the back of a truck, and again I wheeled it into the crowded garage next to its environmentally friendly Frankenstein counterpart.

I stood there with a cold beer looking at the two bikes. Just to know what it felt like I threw a new battery into the spare-parts bike, changed out the spark plug, flushed the lines and carby, cleaned the filters, siphoned out some fuel from one of my other bikes and started it up. The Ducati-built four-stroke 600 single thumped to life; I waited till early the following morning to take it out for a thrashing. It was a good bike—pity I had to pull it apart for parts.

An old oilfield mate, Ross Luck, jumped in with an offer to fabricate the cage to cover the tray. I rolled up with the truck and sat down in his office. Ross doesn't mince his words; he instantly knew what I wanted and began drawing out the finished unit on a pad before I could say, 'Where should I put the fuel cells?' He spaced everything out for optimum weight distribution, and included rubber-lined brackets to brace the fuel cells, and side-lockable ports to pull the bowser-style pump handle through, so I could fill up the bike without having to open up the back of the truck and turn on the pumps. All I would have to do is pull up on the left or right side of the truck, open the port, reach in, flick on the fuel pump, pull out the bowser handle and fill the bike up. 'Don't forget to alternate your sides, so the tanks drain at equal rates,' Ross instructed. He included shelving, and even a special swivel seat that Dan the cameraman could install so he could film safely from the back of the truck. The doors lifted off and stowed down one side. The seat had a heavy welded shaft that slotted into what looked like 3½-inch tubing welded directly to the chassis; it had a safety chain and a four-point harness.

'You could tow another truck from the back of this chair, mate,' said the welder, another Paul. He did a remarkable job; every aspect of Ross's design was faithfully reproduced down to the finest detail. I was overjoyed.

Next I rode Betty to Ross's workshop, and we pushed her up the ramp into the wheel clamp. It was a perfect setup, custom made for the bike. Five minutes later Ross and Paul had pulled the brakes apart and remade them, boosting my angle on the pedal and beefing up the steel. Ross took her for a blat around the block. He came back laughing—he usually gets around on a Harley Night Train. It must have been like sitting on a lawn mower.

Practice makes perfect, provided of course you have the right parts. I drilled myself over and over again on changing tyres, chains, sprockets, filters, the whole lot. Betty and I went for ever longer rides from Perth. I was getting to know her, and discovering that many of her character traits were—how can I put this?—less than ideal. Betty was loud, so loud people walking down the street 50 yards away would turn to see what was making that bizarre noise. This was often followed by an open-mouthed stare and the question: 'Mate, is that thing a diesel?' Riding Betty past a group of people waiting roadside for a bus was a cringe-making, loud, smelly and smoky experience; the combination of her rank green colour, noise and exhaust fumes was as repellent as you could imagine.

I also did my research on riding gear. I was going to encounter rain, wind and temperatures ranging from freezing up to 50 degrees Celsius, so I needed a good full-face helmet, gloves for the cold weather and the heat, fully armoured boots and riding pants. The choice out here is literally mind-numbing and shop assistants do my head in. In the end I settled for a combination of the gear I've always used and trusted and some new gear.

One evening I came home with the CB radio communications, a simple setup consisting of three hand-held CB units. One could be plumbed into the helmet via Velcro flat speakers with a mouthpiece and a small push-to-talk button that would go on the left handlebar grip. There was one unit for the truck driver and one for the cameraman to use when he was in the back of the truck or filming by the side of the road; that way we could all talk to each other all the time. I'm usually one of those guys who has to play with the new thing before examining the instructions. 'RTFM,' Erwin used to say after I'd complained about some new toy not working: Read The Fuckin Manual. This time

I did. Standing on my front lawn in pyjama pants and a new white full-face helmet with carefully attached communication wiring, a shiny new CB radio in my hand, I pressed the push-to-talk button. 'Honey, can you hear me?' Clare was in the living room halfway through another classic episode of *So You Think You're Too Fat?* and wasn't replying. There was nothing, just static. I pressed the button again. 'Hey babe, you hearing me, over?'

Nothing. A bus went past, full of people staring at me. 'Hey love, baby, come in.' I cranked the volume knob. 'Hey baby, I've got my helmet on, can you hear me or what?'

'I CAN HEAR YOU, MATE.' A deep man's voice came booming into my head. I doubled over in pain, fumbling for the volume knob. 'SO WHERE'S YOUR HONEY?'

Clare came on: 'Hi love, over, who was that, was that you?'

'THE NAME'S EARL, SWEETHEART.'

I'd forgotten it was a regular open CB, so anyone on channel 44 or scanning would have heard me. No doubt he was some truckie, probably rolling down the freeway behind our house. 'Arggh, make him go away,' Clare groaned. She was standing at the window laughing at me.

The last few things came together quickly: the tarp to cover the cage, a two-tonne trolley jack, an extra spare wheel for the truck, plus a few small items like a GPS and a mini fridge for the cab. Mates from the oilfield started calling with offers to help, and thanks to them I was able to keep my costs down. Doing some experimental filming, we discovered that Betty's rank lime-green colour was overpowering my sponsors' stickers on screen, so my mate Goldie jumped in with an offer to re-spray her. I had stripped the spares bike by then so he did the whole lot, two black sets of everything, perfect job. Black Betty was reborn with a new diesel heart transplant, ready to take on a whole continent.

11 TO ADELAIDE AND BEYOND

Dan Stevenson, the cameraman, arrived in Perth four days before our scheduled departure. Dan is in his early thirties, and has loads of experience doing this kind of fly-by-the-seat-of-your-pants filming. He's calm, creative and thoughtful but, as I was to find out, very, very forgetful.

I knew everything worked, but what I didn't know was if it would all work together. We needed to practise, Dan in the special filming seat, camera harness and comms on, me riding behind the truck, and both of us in communication with the driver. I called my mate Dave and asked him if he could spare the time to drive the truck all over the place while we got used to the gear. He came straight over. Like most of my mates Dave's an oil man. He's mad on his car, a brand-new Audi R8; the truck must have been punishing for him in comparison.

During our run-through we had a few dramas. At first I couldn't hear Dave but Dan could. Dave would brake while I was too close to the back of the truck and I almost ended up in Dan's lap several times. But eventually we made it work.

The next day I had to drop Ossy the cat off at the cat hotel, his new home for the next three months. We had taken him to the vet a few weeks earlier as he was doing some seriously weird shit. He was starting to look a bit haggard as well, like an elderly bum had just been reborn as a cat. It was $600 worth of blood tests and check-up.

When we returned with Ossy to get the results, the vet gave us that sympathetic smile. Oh dear, I thought, he's gonna give us the sleepy needle speech. But no. Ossy's blood work had come back revealing the bastard was built like a freight train. 'He's a big boy; when he was young he must have looked more like a dog disguised as a cat.' The vet strained to lift Ossy's bulk up onto the counter. 'He's around nineteen, but could last another five years—all his organs are working fine. Considering his history he's in great shape physically, but his hearing is very impaired. Also, his erratic behaviour and night terrors are classic signs of cat dementia.'

Madura Pass, crossing the Nullarbor.

Lola maxing and relaxing in the back of the truck.

Pre-ride anti-vibration training.

Matty's pre-ride survival training.

Gavin Kelly and myself on the Victoria River. We're supposed to be fishing.

Dan Stevenson—full-time camera man, part-time lunatic.

Dan and Dave Henry getting the chopper shot.

Gav making friends with the locals, Bullo River, NT.

It's only bad when they overtake you.

Riding into the sun, central
Queensland.

He died just after I got there.

The bush at dusk—hard to beat.

'So Pauli, how are you feeling?'

Too much glare, do it again. Too much noise, do it again. That truck's in the shot now, do it again. Where did that eagle come from? Do it again. I need to pee, do it again. Where's the long lens? Can you do it again? Okay, almost there, no wait the battery's flat, do it again.

It's a big bite.

Longreach Hospital interview.

Betty's donk now resides in the Australian National Motorcycle Museum.

Betty's big bad sister the high performance diesel motorcycle awaiting final stages of fabrication at the University of Adelaide's Mechanical Engineering Department, ready for a land speed record attempt on the salt flats during Speed Week 2011 at Lake Gairdner.

'What?' I looked down at Ossy. A small string of cat drool was about to connect his head to the countertop.

'Cognitive dysfunction syndrome,' the vet said.

'OK, so he's going mad,' I said.

Clare jumped in. 'He's just an old man, honey.'

The vet smiled and stroked the back of Ossy's head. 'Look, he could settle down or stay the same, or it could get much worse. Just monitor him and come back if you think you need to.' Ossy was now crashed out next to the fax machine on the counter, looking like a bum next to a dumpster. We took him home.

Let me explain what the vet meant by erratic cat behaviour. Ossy would wake up at 2 a.m., walk into our bedroom, come over to my side of the bed and let go with a series of howls that our neighbours could hear. This was dementia cat speak for: 'WHAT THE FUCK AM I DOING HERE? . . . I DON'T KNOW WHO I AM . . . NO, WAIT, I'M A WELDER FROM NEWCASTLE.' I would wake up with a start, and in the meantime Ossy would walk into Lola's room, and let go with another howl—'WHAT THE FUCK'S GOING ON WITH ALL THIS GIANT FURNITURE?'— from directly underneath her cot, so she would start howling too, and now the two tenors would begin their impromptu sold-out concert. Clare and I took it in turns to deal with it.

Calming my daughter down involved the search and retrieval of one of her two compulsory sleep dummies.

She's got a hell of an arm on her, so I never found them in the cot, but on top of her wardrobe or pegged halfway down the hall. While I was rocking her on my shoulder in the dark and looking for said dummy, Oswald would see me, stop mid-howl and say to himself, 'Oh . . . that's right . . . I'm a domestic cat, I live here with this bald idiot and his mental family. Shit, I'm going back to bed.' I've seen his face at this moment; you could see the realisation come crashing down. He'd walk off slowly towards his bed. 'Fucking humans,' he mumbles under his kitty-cat breath. Two hours later the whole thing would start again. 'WHY IS IT DARK? . . . WHO THE FUCK AM I?'

That's not to say he wasn't affectionate, though he chose his moments. One night, after working on the bike till very late, I found myself asleep on the toilet at 3 a.m. I woke up, my eyes struggling to focus, and looked down to see the old cat curled up in the nest of jocks and trousers between my ankles, his bulky frame spilling over the edges and his drool everywhere.

So you'll likely sympathise when I say I had a twang of separation anxiety as I pulled away from the cat hotel. Even in the car with the aircon on and the engine running, I could hear Ossy protesting from his new digs. The cats next door to his fenced room were considerably smaller than him, and they all had the same reaction to his arrival, scooting off to hide under their beds. I hoped the crazy old bastard would still be around when I got back.

I could hardly believe it was 1 August 2009, but the time had finally come. Dan was ready to film us leaving. He would then fly back to Sydney and six days later come to Adelaide with 200 pounds of filming gear, ready to spend the next three months on the road with me, poor bastard. I had a good feeling about Dan: he could go the distance, and most importantly he had a great sense of humour.

Now he quietly went about assembling his huge pile of kit while we ran around trying not to forget things. One of the last-minute jobs was properly tethering Lola's baby seat to the back seat of the truck. There was a portable DVD player mounted behind the driver's headrest so she could watch her movies and hopefully not scream the cab down all the way to Adelaide. By mid-morning we finally had everything squared away. The truck was clean and organised, with everything in its place, everything accounted for and working. I would never see it like that again.

This was it: departure time. I wasn't going to see my home again until I rode Betty through Perth on the way back to Adelaide. Our neighbours came out to see us off. Nick and and Gorga are great people, we're lucky to have such a cool couple living next door. They would keep an eye on our place while we were away, empty the letterbox, mow the lawn—the usual stuff. Nick and I had sat in his backyard the night before, drinking whisky and talking till late. He's a good laugh, always the optimist. 'Don't worry about the house, mate, we're going to turn it into a roller disco next week, I'm gonna flog your bikes and have sweet rave parties in your garage.'

Right, had I thought of everything? I went through my list, mentally ticking things off in my head. Standing on my driveway, the sun beating down on me, I knew that everything that could be done, had been done. Lola was in her seat already plugged into The Wiggles, Clare was hugging Gorga, and Dan was standing on our front lawn patiently holding his camera. I was ready, the truck was full of fuel, spare tyres, food, water, the sat phone, CB radio, sat nav, and enough spare parts and tools to give MacGyver a boner.

Finally, the first part of this journey was beginning. As we pulled out into our quiet street, I felt my sense of adventure flare up; my pilot light was back on.

Perth's suburbs drained away fast. Clare and I talked and talked, our conversation going all over the place. Before long we had trundled past Southern Cross. We both stopped talking simultaneously at the crest of a hill. The straight road rolled under the truck's cab in silence. Ahead, blacktop line into infinity. The heat haze washed it with mercury silver sheen. Even though it was bumpy and we were doing 110 kilometres an hour it felt like we were standing still. 'Shit babe, it's a long way to Adelaide,' Clare said, turning to check on our daughter. The Wiggles had put Lola out cold in the back.

I know about riding a bike in the heat, but driving an air-conditioned truck at the speed limit is an entirely different experience. Betty was going to be the slowest thing on the road and that would be frustrating and dull. Plus riders like corners and hills, and the Great Eastern Highway is short on both.

We rolled into Norseman that evening off the Coolgardie–Esperance Highway, checked into a motel, and all three of us fell into a vast still sleep; the 700 k's had zapped our energy. In the morning Clare got the coffee going while Lola climbed onto my chest and prised open an eyelid. 'Cheeky Daddy,' she said. I had to get up and start the day. After a daybreak roadhouse breakfast, a refuel, and a quick check of oil, water, tyre pressure, we hit the road again.

If I'd thought the previous day was a dull prospect for a motorcyclist, well, the second day was worse. The Eyre Highway was the road equivalent of a doctor's waiting room without the two-year-old copies of *Woman's Day*.

We stopped to refuel in Balladonia; Lola made friends with a puddle of diesel—clearly she's my daughter— and then we spent half an hour cleaning her up. We ate petrol station sandwiches that had an interesting diesel aftertaste, and climbed aboard for more of the same. This particular stretch of the Eyre Highway, around 150 k's, is Australia's longest straight road. I was so happy to have my girls there with me; doing this journey by myself would have been painful otherwise. There were some drawbacks though. Lola by now had watched *Finding Nemo* close to six times and she was nowhere near bored with it. As a consequence, Clare and I can recite that entire movie verbatim—that, and we know every song in The Wiggles' repertoire.

Somewhere between the end of the long straight bit and our destination for the night at Madura Pass, Lola had a massive freakout. She went from fast asleep to ballistic in a nanosecond. I would ordinarily just put this down to what we had heard other parents describe as the 'terrible twos'—those times when your sweet little toddler is smiling and chatting one minute, and seconds later is possessed and biting, arms thrashing wildly. Our little girl is no exception: I was starting to consider shaving her head to look for the three sixes. But this time I could sympathise with her.

We pulled over and discovered her slumber had been disturbed by a cockroach. It had probably crawled into our open cooler bag last night in the motel. While Lola was passed out in front of *Finding Nemo*, the insect had made an attempt at circumnavigating the top of her head. Now, Lola's usually unfazed by insects, and picking them up for a closer inspection is normal. This often progresses into a simple hand crush to see what they look like on the inside, or she goes full Bear Grylls mode and just flat-out eats them, with all Bear's facial expressions. (We love watching Bear Grylls' TV show *Man vs Wild*; Lola in particular loves it, especially when Mr Edward Grylls eats insects.) However, this was her first contact with a cockroach. She had woken up, managed to grab the beasty, and then gone bananas.

It appeared that along with a love of diesel and axle bolts, Lola could have inherited my fear of cockroaches. We all have a thing, don't we? You might be freaked by snakes or rats or sharks, but my freakout is the humble roach, closely followed by spiders. I can deal with everything else, and over the last twenty years I've woken up in various Third World jungles to find all manner of beasties biting, burrowing or feeding on me, both externally and internally. But it was a cockroach that caused my record freakout.

After my wife had dealt with the roach, we climbed back into the cab and pushed on. Clare was laughing, clearly reminiscing about a horrible moment in my past. 'I'll never forget that night . . .' She smiled at me sympathetically.

'Hmm.' I shifted uncomfortably behind the wheel and started brushing off imaginary roaches.

Four years earlier I was working a rotation in Japan, on a land rig in Hokkaido. I had just flown back into Australia for my days off, ready to have some fun. We had accepted an invitation to spend a night at a friend's parents' holiday home an hour out of Sydney. Simon and Sally are always a great laugh, so Clare and I were really looking forward to a good catch up, no doubt an excellent meal, and some very fine wine. Our evening unfolded as expected. Simon cooked, Sally had me laughing so much I got hiccups, we all hammered the wine and ate too much, and ended up around a huge fireplace with Simon's 25-year-old single malt before wandering off to bed at midnight, happily pissed.

The house was massive, and our room was on the ground floor, near the kitchen. I was still pissed but woke suddenly in fright, kicking the covers off the bed. I can't remember much about it, but Clare said I was on all fours and completely rigid, my eyes wide in panic.

'There's something in my head,' I apparently screamed.

Right, so you get the picture. She's thinking, 'Oh perfect, now I find out he's actually completely mental.' I'm still blurry on this part, but somehow she ascertained that I wasn't having a psychotic episode.

I was by now rolling about on the floor, both hands cupped over my head, demanding something I could poke into my left ear. My frantic wife took off down the hall, doing the Tom Cruise sock slide into Simon's parents' holiday home kitchen where she started madly riffling through drawers. I was by now completely sober and in ridiculous amounts of pain. The horrible realisation that something had crawled right into my ear, and was now attempting to burrow through my eardrum and into my brain, was making me crazy.

Clare burst into the bedroom with a meat skewer in her hand. 'WHAT THE FUCK BABE, I'M NOT

JAMMING THAT FUCKING THING INTO MY EAR,' I screamed. I was convulsing and slapping my hand against the left side of my head. The insect or whatever it was seemed intent on moving forward. It was, in a word, terrifying.

'CALM DOWN, I NEED TO WAKE UP SALLY,' Clare shouted at me. I must have looked out of my mind, because she took off again. She reappeared next to me with a fistful of uncooked spaghetti, and was off up the stairs to wake our hosts.

I shoved the end of a stick of the spaghetti into my ear. This made whatever was in there only more determined. I could feel lots of sharp legs madly scrambling, and every few seconds something hit my eardrum. You know when you're fiddling about in your ear with a Q-Tip and you push it in just a bit too far, and it bloody hurts? Right, well imagine hitting the end of that with a hammer, and that's what it felt like. I was beside myself with fear, pain and spaghetti. Simon and Sal came running in, wearing what looked like each other's underwear. 'Jump in the car mate,' Simon said, trying to sound sober.

I ran out to the dark winter driveway, twitching wildly. Sally rang ahead to tell the local emergency room there was a disturbed bald man in his underwear about to arrive with something digging a hole through his head.

The drive was only a few miles, but it might as well have been to the moon as far as I was concerned. Panic started to shoot waves of adrenalin through my body as we pulled into the small hospital, the two main doors and big red emergency sign flooding the car park in fluorescent light. Simon leaped from the car and ran inside. Clare opened the car door for me and I sprang into the cold like a wild man. The doctor on duty that night was waiting just inside the entrance; he simply gestured me towards an open doorway. Clare sat down in the waiting room with Simon, who looked drunk but appropriately concerned.

I stood in the little examination room staring at the eye chart on the opposite wall and nervously hopping from toe to toe while the doctor sauntered in and casually closed the door, regarding me with a whimsical look. 'Right, you've got an insect in your ear then.'

I twitched, my eyes big and crazy. I closed the gap between us, put both hands on his shoulders. 'Get it out, for fuck's sake.'

He straightened up instantly, all humour gone. 'Don't worry, Mr Carter. Over to the bed and sit down, please.'

I leaped onto the bed. 'Call me Paul. Just get it out, Doc.'

He produced one of those black trumpet-shaped scope things with the little light, pulled down on my lobe and poked in the scope. As his head drew close to the lens he jerked back. 'Whoa,' was all I heard.

'What the fuck is it?' I asked.

He put down the scope. 'Well, there's a big cockroach in there, but don't worry, first we're going to drown him with oil, then we can remove him.'

'Whaddya mean *drown* him? It doesn't need to look like an accident—why don't you send in a hit man? Drown him in oil, what do you mean in oil? I work in oil. What kind of oil? Why fuck about with a drowning? Just use a gun—even better, there's a meat skewer back at the house . . .' I was raving, but he was already gone. I sat there for what seemed like forever. My new friend, sensing he was in real trouble, began scratching around even harder. The doc came back with a giant turkey baster full of warm vegetable oil. He had to sit on my head to keep me still while a nurse squirted the oil into my ear.

The roach went into his death throes while he slowly suffocated. The doc held on while I screamed and bucked wildly. The nurse held the examination bed down while the doc enjoyed his first human-head rodeo; he rode for the full eight seconds before dismounting and straightening out his hair. I lay there twitching in unison with my newly drowned friend.

His oil-covered cadaver came out in two pieces. Rejoined, he was an inch long. I took him back to the house in a bio-hazard container to show everyone.

Just before I went back to the rig, Clare and I were getting ready for bed and I wandered into the bedroom and stretched out on top of the bed. Just as she came in and turned off the light a Bondi roach flew through the open window like a bronzed hockey puck with wings, and landed on my chest. I lost him behind the wardrobe twenty minutes and several failed attempts to kill him later. Sleep came eventually after stuffing my ears full of toilet paper.

Back on the road to Adelaide, we made regular stops to stretch our legs and point at nothing. The odd dingo mooched about looking for a handout. There was a roadhouse every 200 kilometres or so. Clare fell asleep; Lola was still fixated on *Finding Nemo* and I let my mind wander. There was going to be a lot of this to come, I thought. It's a hard barren place out there. I don't know what triggered it, but having my girls in that truck with me sparked my instinct to protect them. The sky turned to stone as dusk approached, then from nowhere it started pouring with rain.

We ascended through the Madura Pass at nightfall, with rain still falling hard, and pulled up at the motel there. 'Try the quiche, it's really good,' said the motel manager as I checked us in. I glanced over to the driveway; Clare was waking up in the cab outside.

The manager was a big man with a shaved head, a goatee and a lazy eye. On a night like this one, my first impression was that he had probably just finished digging three shallow graves out in the bush in anticipation of our arrival. It didn't help that the motel was a big spread-out complex at the base of the pass. Other than us and the manager, it appeared to be totally empty. Our room was at the end of a wing that stretched into darkness.

'This place is creepy,' said Clare, looking through the rain as lightning lit up the wet landscape.

We unloaded our bags and ran back to the main building for something to eat. The motel manager was there. 'Try the quiche,' he grinned. 'It's really good.'

We sat there in the restaurant alone, not another soul in there. 'This place is like an Aussie Bates Motel,' I whispered.

Clare looked worried and put on Lola's bib. 'He's scary,' she said.

'Are you going to have the quiche? Apparently it's really good.'

She pulled a face. The manager returned a moment later with a pad.

'I'll have the quiche,' I said, smiling at Clare. Clare had a salad and Lola demolished a big piece of fish.

The quiche was horrible, our night was long, the door had a flimsy lock on it, and Clare was convinced the motel manager was going to burst through the door and hack us up with a fire axe. She was ready to pile up the furniture against the door, but in the end the night was uneventful. The manager was in fact a perfect gentleman with a dry sense of humour and bad taste in quiche.

We crossed the border into South Australia the next day. I watched an electrical storm brewing over the Bunda Cliffs on the northern side of the road, rain cascading down in liquid sheets across the highway and out to the southern ocean.

The rest of our journey played out in much the same way, with two more days of driving. Crossing the Nullarbor Plain is, well ... plain, especially the part called the Treeless Plain—that's *really* plain. But eventually the plain gave way to grassy rolling hills and the outskirts of Adelaide.

12 STAGE ONE: GREEN FUEL, WHITE KNUCKLES

I hadn't really slept the night before, but day one, stage one, had me out of the hotel at 6 a.m. and over to the uni's workshop. Howard, the support driver, was due to arrive in an hour, and then we had to get the truck over to the MoGas holding yard and fill up the tanks with 800 litres of bio-fuel that had been waiting there for me for weeks. Then all we'd have to do was wait for the lord mayor and the media to arrive before we could take off. At 6.30 a.m. I stood there in the workshop with a mug of coffee, the huge roller door opened to a big, almost empty car park surrounded on three sides by the university's buildings. The truck was parked next to Betty, and everything was packed, ready to go. Only a few people were around; it was the calm before the storm. I had the time and the quiet to reflect on the last four months.

What was I really trying to do, I wondered, other than ride a bike around Australia (which had been done many times before?). Well, it was the fuel and the bike that made this ride different, and that was the bit that excited me. The uni had built Betty as a prototype, but Colin and his students hoped that once this ride was over, she could be used as an example, perhaps in a first tentative step towards the production of an Australian-made motorcycle for the farming community to use on their properties, powered by the same diesel fuel used in tractors, pumps and all manner of motorised farming machines. As with any other ag bike which would only be used on a farm, it wouldn't have to be registered to run on the road. More ambitiously, though, this first-generation agricultural motorcycle could run just as effectively on bio-fuel. Every rural community has a roadhouse or a pub that each week discards around 20 litres of used cooking oil. One roadhouse could provide enough fuel to run one bike for over 500 kilometres of travel a week. I had discovered in the course of my research that the farming community in Australia is more than willing to embrace the concept of a bio-fuel ag bike, as for many farmers the cost of running a standard fossil-fuel-burning quad bike, in terms of fuel and maintenance, is on par with running a car. Fuel is one of their biggest costs.

And then there was its potential application in the city. Could you imagine all those people who ride cheap scooters to work every day instead riding a version of Betty to the office, no longer paying for their fuel at the service station in the city? Though the loss in fuel tax revenue alone would have the bike taxed in some other way before it even left the factory. Bio-fuel could also have applications in public transport or industry.

Transport contributes some 16 per cent of Australia's greenhouse gas emissions. Seventeen per cent of that is from the burning of diesel fuel. Fuels made from used vegetable and animal fats are renewable, and the costs involved in production are very moderate; production of bio-fuel, called transesterification, is not a hard process. When bio-fuel is used it produces 60 per cent less carbon monoxide and total hydrocarbons than fossil fuels. It's also non-toxic to animals or marine life. If there was ever a spill, after three weeks it would degrade to sugars and starches; it's ten times less toxic than table salt.

No, this wasn't just another adventure. This entire project revolved around the effective use of waste cooking oil, and it was crucial that I didn't fuck it up. There was a lot riding on this, apart from my arse; it wasn't just about me getting from point A to point B and having my jollies. There was a purpose to it, and a responsibility as well. I drained my coffee, feeling good about the prospect of getting on the road.

Rob and Steve, the workshop guys, arrived. They gave me a supportive slap on the back and wished me luck. Rob even lent me his personal generator and a full jerry can of fuel. Howard called from the airport; he was on the way. The lord mayor's office called to tell me the TV networks and press were also inbound, as was the lord mayor. Last and most importantly, my wife and daughter were on their way. It was time.

Howard got there first, followed by Dan. We jumped into the cab and we headed off to pick up the fuel. You'd think getting the fuel would be relatively simple, but no. We got lost on the way—incidentally, our directions included a line that said we had to turn right at a sex shop, brilliantly called Beaver World—and then I had a freakout when we got to the bio-fuel storage yard and discovered that the fuel was kept in a special vessel and my tanks were bolted to the floor in the back of the truck, and there was no way of connecting one with the other. I didn't have a hand pump or any hose or funnels to transfer the fuel into my tanks; conscious of time ticking on and the assembling media, I started to sweat. Howard, being calm and capable, had a scout around and soon came back with funnels and a hose. We picked up the vessel using the on-site forklift, plumbed in the hose he'd found and funnelled fuel into one tank, then transferred fuel over into the other tank using the internal pump. Perfect.

We got back to the workshop, where Howard put on the CB headset. I got on Betty, continuing to talk to him over the radio. Colin gave me the nod; we had to drive around the corner and pull up out the front of the uni where I was to chat to the media people, shake the lord mayor's hand, kiss my wife and daughter goodbye and peel off into the waiting city like a bio-fuel poster boy.

And, thank Christ, that's exactly how it went. It was a perfect departure, all smiles and camera flashes, proud wife holding waving baby daughter, cue wind tussle of hair as wife looks happy but concerned.

But just two blocks down the road I stopped, realising I'd just spent half an hour telling the country's media that people could check out the journey online by going to www.thegoodoil.tv, yet this website was not emblazoned on the truck, or anywhere else for that matter. How did I miss that? So we detoured to the nearest Bunning's and picked up some stick-on letters and fixed up my mistake.

Our first night's stop was due to be Mount Gambier via Keith. My initial joy at finally being on the road was ephemeral to say the least. The first thing that hit me—again—was how slow Betty was. The second thing that hit me—on a highway surrounded by trucks—was the shockwave of wind right after each truck has shot past. My hands were totally numb from the vibrations coming through the bars. Now that's a weird feeling: you know you're holding onto the handlebars, you just can't feel it.

Betty's riding dynamic was like no other bike I'd ridden. She didn't like hills and hated cross-winds.

I had experienced this before but this was fairly tough riding. The Coonawarra hammered me with a sudden freezing wind, blowing the bike all over the place. When the sun started to set the temperature plummeted, the wind picked up again and the rain set in. We were only halfway to Mount Gambier, and I was getting fatigued and a little scared at the thought of riding at night, when Betty's CVT belt suddenly let go. We pulled over by the side of the highway. The trucks shooting past kept knocking Betty over, so I decided to ride her up the ramp into the back of the truck where I could put her in the wheel brace and work on her out of the wind.

That was my first mistake. I had previously ridden her successfully up the ramp at home; you needed a good run-up as she didn't have the torque to get up without it. But with all my riding gear and a full tank of fuel she was so heavy that the bottom of the frame slammed into the back of the truck when I got to the top of the ramp. I fell backwards, the bike landing unceremoniously next to me, smashing its tail-light and indicators. With me in the back seat of the truck, we pulled into Mount Gambier late that night. Howard crashed; I had a whisky and moaned to Dan for an hour about being a shit rider.

I crawled out of bed at 5 a.m. and spent two hours fixing the tail-light and indicators and replacing the CVT drive belt. Dan was late getting up. I didn't know it yet, but Dan is not a morning person: he likes a lie-in. Before the week was up Howard had renamed him Mattress Man. Poor Dan: half-man, half-bed.

We fuelled up, pigged out, coffee'd up, and took off into another cold wet day. Next stop was Melbourne, and we had two days there to figure out how I was going to make this bike go all the way round the continent without it killing me. Twenty minutes after setting off we crossed into Victoria. I wouldn't see South Australia again for over three months—that is, if I ever saw it again.

We stopped briefly in Warrnambool, where I pulled on a few more layers. During the following leg frustration really kicked in. Bike after bike flew past me on the Great Ocean Road; *everyone* flew past me, even little doddery grannies in ten-year-old Honda Civics with their noses one inch from the windscreen. I got abused by all of them because I was so slow. They could not understand why this guy on a big motorcycle was only doing 80 kilometres per hour. I was in the slow lane, where you can legally do 80, but this just wasn't good enough for the average mild-mannered motorist, most of whom simply defaulted to giving me the finger and/or a verbal serve on passing.

I'd had enough, so we turned off the coastal route at Lavers Hill, heading northeast. This country was much better for an underpowered bike. Betty cruised over the Otway Ranges through some really pretty country. The sun came out, the road traffic was light and I started to enjoy myself—that is, until the sun went down and we hit the Princes Highway. Back to the road rage and abuse—again with the hand gestures—from fast-moving cars; trucks blew by threatening to suck me from the handlebars. It was impatient driving at its worst. One bloke even threw a kebab at me.

We finally hit the last long artery that would plug us into Melbourne. The sun had well and truly set behind me. All I had to do was hold the throttle open and avoid getting pummelled in the traffic. At one point we traversed a series of big hills that came out into a huge sweeping run; the wind suddenly picked up on the eastern side and got behind me, and the highway fell away, descending sharply out in front as far as I could see. Betty hit a ton and I was happy. Tucked in behind her fairing, I optimistically changed into the middle lane for the first time since leaving Adelaide. Betty cracked 110, and I started ranting, 'LOOK AT ME FLY NOW, YOU FUCKING WANKERS.'

Howard got on the radio. 'Pauli mate, did you pull over? We can't see you.'

I started overtaking the left lane. Kebab guy in his big manly red penis of a ute was in the right lane ahead of me, but was now stuck behind a truck. Betty hit 125; I couldn't believe it.

'Pauli, come back, over.' Howard sounded concerned. 'Where are you, mate? Over.'

I pressed the little red transmit button on the left grip. 'I'M DOING 130 K'S MATE, THIS HILL AND THE WIND, AWESOME—130! OVER.'

Howard came back on the radio, laughing. 'Just keep going, we'll catch up.'

I shifted my weight back and lay over the tank, tucking in my legs and elbows. She was still picking up speed—I stared at the speedo: 140 now—her wild vibration making the front end speed-wobble. Ute guy was level on my right side. He heard the tiny diesel engine shrieking in agony next to his phallic red turd. I was getting close to losing control of Betty; her vibrations were so intense my bum skipped forward on the seat.

'ONE HUNDRED AND FORTY ON COOKING OIL AND AN EIGHT-HORSEPOWER PUMP ENGINE, YEAHHHHH.'

He looked over, and his jaw dropped open.

'FUCK YOU, CUNT.' I gave him the finger with my left hand; my right hand was holding the throttle on full and completely numb. In fact, both my arms were completely dead from the elbow down, and I realised I was waving my index finger at kebab guy. He gave me a quizzical look, leaned forward in his nice warm comfortable seat to see what I was pointing at, then returned me the finger, stomped his foot into the firewall and disappeared, just as Betty's CVT belt flew apart again.

It was freezing cold as we crossed over the Bolte Bridge into Melbourne much later that night. I was in the middle lane following Howard; he was acting as a weather shield. The traffic was horrendous, bumper to bumper; I was boxed in between a bus on my left, a cab on my right, and a semi right on my arse. I heard the truck getting close. I fired a quick look over my shoulder—the bastard was two feet from my back wheel, all I could see in the mirror was chrome grille. Howard could also see what was going on. 'Pauli, how close is that truck?'

I was waving my left hand at the cab asking him to back off. 'Too fuckin close mate, I'm boxed in.' This was getting really frightening.

We reached the highest point of the bridge, hundreds of feet up in the air, the cross-wind buffeting Betty, when the big truck applied the pressure again. I looked back: he was right there on top of me. I turned my radio over to channel 44, the one the truckies use. 'Hey, truck on my arse halfway over the Bolte Bridge, back off.'

He came back to me straightaway: 'Get out of the way then.'

'I'VE GOT NOWHERE TO GO. NOW BACK OFF MATE, THIS IS DANGEROUS.'

Howard managed to pull into the right lane and slow down, creating a gap for me to cross into and get out of this idiot's way. It was right at that moment that Betty started coughing and lost power.

I pulled into the right lane just in time. It was so close, I thought the truck was going to go straight over the top of me. If Howard had not acted when he did and made that gap, I would have been stuffed.

'GET THE NUMBER, GET THE NUMBER,' I screamed over the radio. I was ready to kill that guy, no question.

A few seconds later, Betty's power came back; I didn't know why it had dropped out—could have been a blocked fuel line or a clogged injector. We descended into the city. I was fizzing, full of adrenalin, but it passed. The safety of the city streets put me at ease.

I had rented a small terrace house in Richmond for three nights, only a block from my mate James' Supercar Club building. He had offered me some space to work on the bike, so I could spread out all my tools and take my time. However, I had not been able to raise him on the phone over the last few days. As it turned out he was overseas, so we made straight for the rental house. I was shattered.

The tiny garage had once been full-size but had been converted into a bedroom; only the first metre was still garage, and it now housed a small laundry and two bins. There was a door leading from the garage into the bedroom, so we just opened it and parked Betty half-in, half-out of the room. Howard and Dan were as tired as I was, so we all had a beer together then called it a night—but not before I made a call on that truck.

Melbourne is a wonderful city, and we had two days to relax. Howard had to bolt first thing in the morning; he was moving house the next day and his wife didn't like the idea of tackling that alone with two girls under five in tow. He jumped into a taxi, job done; I couldn't thank him enough.

Dan has mates in Melbourne so he was off as well, intent on chasing all the things that a young single man chases on weekend pass. I pulled the tools out of the truck and lay in the street under Betty to do an oil change. The radio in the truck was on, the city came to life as the sun rose over the terraces, and people ambled past with strollers and dogs. Oil change done I replaced the CVT belt, then worked on the rest of the bike, which took up most of the day. That night I went out for dinner with my mates in Melbourne, the Jacobson boys (of *Kenny* fame) and their wives. As always, the two brothers had me in stitches, and the night was over way too fast.

The next day Shane Edwards arrived, full of energy and boundless enthusiasm. Shane does marathons and triathlons and jogs every morning. He eats right, works hard—a real clean-cut Eddie who never has a bad word to say about anyone. But that boy can drink . . . 'Let's get on it,' were the first words out of his mouth.

'Er, OK,' I said, and we went straight to the pub, where two of his mates joined us.

Ten hours later Fast Eddie was walking on footballs and slurring his words, as we discussed whether to go clubbing or move on to another pub. We were in the corner of a pub somewhere in the city, a nice place, not too crowded for a Saturday night. 'WHHOOOO,' Eddie said suddenly, with his arms in the air, 'we're going to the Black Spurrr, me laddy.' He raised his eyebrows to emphasise this and grinned.

'What's the Black Spur?' I asked. 'And why are you talking like a pirate?'

Eddie's mates picked up on the pirate thing. 'Beware the Spur boy, it'll swallow ye up like a prawn, so it will, arrr.'

I started laughing. Eddie was on fire; he stood up and did a little drunk jig. 'The Black Spur be no place for a bio-gay bike and a baldy-headed fool. Lucky for you I'm just the man te get ya there, 'n no bones about it.' He flopped back into his seat and laughed.

'OK lads, what the fuck is the Black Spur?'

'BEWARE THE BLACK SPUR,' they all joined in.

I finished my drink. 'It's just a hill mate, the black spur,' said Eddie. 'BEWARE THE . . .'

'SHUT THE FUCK UP.'

'That bike is never going to get up it. Let's get a taco.'

Our night went on into the morning. At one point Dan called me; he was as smashed as I was and wanted to meet up with us at some club but that was never going to happen. Eddie, his mates and I ended up in a random horrid little bar, more like a public toilet with a bouncer; from the smell of the place it was bang in the middle of Melbourne's urine district. I spent an hour doing shooters and sticking to the carpet.

When we got back to the house, I was worried about the truck getting tagged by some kids we'd passed on the corner, so I went out to move it closer to the house. Bad move. My attempt to drive twenty metres down the road started and finished with the truck lurching forward straight into a streetlight, and that's where I woke up several hours later.

13 STAGE TWO: SPIDERS

Bags packed, our laundry done, a decent breakfast, the bill paid: it was time to depart Melbourne and make for Sydney via Canberra.

'All set, mate.' Eddie looked and sounded like he hadn't even sniffed a drink last night. Bastard. Dan looked the opposite, just like I did. I filled up the bike, pulling the hose through the little flap on the side and flicking on the fuel pump; the smell made me gag.

'What was all that pirate talk about last night?' asked Dan. 'I called you to see if you guys wanted to join me and all I got was "Arrr this" and "the Black Spur that".'

'BEWARE THE BLACK SPUR,' yelled Eddie from the cab. I shot him a smile. 'Pauli spent the night in the truck, it smells like a brewery in here,' said Eddie.

Dan looked puzzled. 'What happened?'

Eddie described my drunken mission to rescue the truck from some taggers.

Dan looked at me. 'It's still parked in the same spot.'

'Not quite.' Eddie pointed at the front left side. 'He managed to shift it all of five feet into that streetlight.' Dan walked around to the other side and started laughing.

Not too much damage, just a dented ego.

The rain started as we pulled off and kept on going for the rest of the day. My head was thumping in perfect time with Betty's donk. I sat behind the truck for ages, riding on autopilot, until we hit Healesville. *Whap, whap, whap.* Sports bikes blasted past us as we began to climb. This must be the start of the dreaded Betty-crushing Black Spur, I thought.

Eddie swiftly confirmed this over the two-way. 'THE BLACK SPUR,' he announced. 'You're never gonna make it, sucka.' I overtook the truck and put-putted into the most amazing high country forest. Two brand spanking KTMs pulled alongside and Betty got the once-over. There was some pointing, lots of laughing, then they barked the engines, down a gear on the throttle, front wheels effortlessly airborne—wankers— and off up the straight on the balance point through the gearbox.

I couldn't do that; I just didn't have the power or the gearbox. But I could enjoy the scenery, hairpin after hairpin straight up into the Yarra Ranges. Betty was doing about twenty kilometres an hour, much to the annoyance of all the cars behind me, but there was nowhere to pull over with any degree of safety.

The ride down the other side was a joy, all the same swervery but no longer underpowered so I could finally keep up with all the other bikes enjoying the run. The KTM duo were stuck behind a caravan, deep in conversation, doing twenty. I thumped past, rushing a really silly overtake on the apex of a right hander—no oncoming traffic but an overhanging tree nearly took my head off. Don't look back, just hold her wide open and go.

The game was on. I caught flashes of their headlights in my mirrors; Betty's footpegs touched bitumen for the first time. I rode as hard and fast as the bike would let me. We duelled, always within our lanes, measured, experienced fun, ripping through turn after turn, the bikes well over, jittery on the lean from the leaf litter on the roadside, into the centre line and back, always thinking ahead, always looking towards the exit point and the next setup. No looking back, or they'd know I was trying, no glancing down at gauges or mirrors. We were flying. At the first straight section we came to the duo pulled up, one on either side of me. I was hopelessly out-gunned, out-wheelied and out-braked. We rode on, three in a row down the straight, no hard-faced manly nods or piss taking, just big happy grins.

'Nice one, mate,' said KTM One; thumbs-up and he was gone.

'It's a diesel, hey?' KTM Two asked.

'Yeah.' I smiled.

'Where you headed?'

'Doing the big lap,' I said.

His eyes widened. 'Really? You're game. Good luck.'

'Cheers,' I said.

He lifted the front end again and blasted away in a spectacular display of proper motorcycle hoonability. Melburnians are truly blessed to have such a great choice of rides to occupy their weekends. Eddie was smiling when we stopped at the bottom.

'Mate, how good was that?' I couldn't stop grinning.

We sat on the Maroondah Highway headed for a small town called Taggerty, where Eddie grew up. 'Mum and Dad's is next, mate, there's gonna be a good feed on.' He sounded excited to be visiting home.

As predicted, Eddie's folks were hospitable beyond words. Dan and I pigged out on Eddie's mum's lasagne, then we got the tour of the property. Eddie's dad, Murray, is the area's deputy group officer, a volunteer firefighter. He casually walked me through a shed to rival my father-in-law's. Guys from that generation know how a man's shed should be: no comfy seats, no designer shelving or super clean floors, just tools—heavily used tools. Power tools, tools with big engines, half a tractor here, half a big-block V8 there, and in the corner an old fridge that looks like a car door packed with man beer, not imported Italian stuff. These men have the man caves that my generation should aspire to. Murray talked casually about the Black Saturday fires that ravaged the area one year before, Australia's worst fire disaster. As he talked, I got a glimpse of the type of men he and Eddie are, just flat-out hard-working, decent blokes who will risk their lives to save people and property from turning to ashes.

Everyone else headed inside for a cuppa and I went to check Betty's almost shredded CVT belt. She was going through these drive belts at an increasingly rapid rate. I wandered through the shed, straight into a waiting spider's web the size of a bed sheet. At the last nanosecond I saw the spider, right in the middle; he looked like he could bench press Spiderman. And right there in the semi-dark wooden shed I did what my wife calls 'the spider dance'—the interpretive instant spin/strip that you do while hopping up and down and wildly rubbing your hands over your head. You know he's holding on somewhere, ready to plunge his white-hot fangs into you. Thank God no one was around to see me do the spider dance—except the spider, of course.

After lunch, we ambled on from Taggerty past Bonnie Doon, made famous in the film *The Castle*, but the lake was dry. We stopped to refuel the truck in Benalla, passed Wangaratta, then got on a minor road to Wodonga on the Victoria/New South Wales border. This little back road was almost as direct a route as the

Hume Highway, and there were no trucks or hell-for-leather near-death experiences. I was back to riding relaxed again; my only lingering worry was the CVT belts—I had only one left.

We crossed the border into New South Wales at dusk, Eddie leading, and got a bit lost looking for the motel in Albury. 'I'm chuckin a uey at the lights, mate,' he said over the radio, while in the background the GPS in a clipped English accent said, 'Execute a legal u-turn at this intersection.' I watched Eddie take out a traffic-light shroud with the side of the truck as he turned around. It rattled down onto the road, so I hopped off and picked it up. I had an old milk crate strapped to the back of the bike where I put my helmet and gloves whenever we stopped, as the wind had been blowing my kit all over the place. Eddie's carnage was placed in there, and I caught up with him still looking for the motel.

'Mate, you nailed that traffic light back there,' I laughed over the radio.

'Bullshit,' said Eddie, so I pulled up next to him waving the shroud at the driver's window. 'Oh shit.' He looked worried.

We found our digs for the night and I was asleep before my head hit the pillow.

New South Wales is my old stomping ground; there's some great riding in this state, but on this trip, it was only on the downhill side. The next day we were off to our nation's capital Canberra, again taking the back roads. We left Albury via the Murray Valley into Corryong, a nice little goldrush town, and then into a valley.

The road was empty so I had a chance to take in the landscape. Shadows spread across the road, and the place felt palpably creepy. 'Good location for a horror film,' Dan said over the radio. He wanted to stop and do some filming against this backdrop. Five takes and ten passes later he was happy.

The road snaked round the foothills of the Snowy Ranges and on to Tumut, then we doubled back on the highway, heading south through Kosciuszko National Park and Australia's highest town, Kiandra. We took a left turn at Cooma and then drove back up north towards Canberra. The day's riding was spectacular. I felt light and happy. It had been a risk, I guess, to ride so far with only one belt left, but the riding was worth it.

About an hour before Canberra we pulled over for a break. I brewed up some tea and lay back under a tree, looking up at the branches swaying. Dan found inspiration in the landscape and bounded off with his stills camera. Eddie was in good form, so we fell into conversation. Before I realised it, we'd burned too much daylight and it was late afternoon.

Off again, me in front this time, and I focused on the road ahead, the bike thumping down the highway. And that's when I felt it. Only a little at first, a light pressure at the back of my head, and then the horror set in. It was like a small hand slowly crawling from the back of my lid to the front. Something big and hairy with long legs was inside my helmet, looking for an exit point.

I checked my rear and slammed on the brakes, locking up the back wheel. A blue streak smoked off the burning rubber as the bike slid off the road. I sprang off, letting the bike fall over like a doddery toddler, and did the Roadside, One-Night-Only, Helmet Spider Dance. It's not unlike the standard spider dance, but this one involves the high-speed removal of gloves and a mad thrashing at the chin strap, followed by helmet soccer and the traditional rubbing of hands over your head.

The truck pulled up just as I was composing myself. Eddie wound down his window. 'Everything OK, mate?' He looked over at the bike lying on its side, the motor running.

'Oh yeah, fine.' I ran over and stood Betty up, smiling at the boys.

We continued on. It was getting dark and really cold, just above freezing; I was wearing all my gear now, almost too many layers to do up the zipper on my jacket. I ran out of fuel less than a kilometre from the motel. Running out of fuel is a prick on Betty; she's hard to start in the cold, and even harder to start with the lines and filter empty.

Canberra was a dark, empty meat locker. We found our motel eventually. I left my bike-maintenance ritual for the morning; it was too dark, too cold, and besides, Eddie had bought beer.

The sun broke through the next morning while I was working on the bike. My last CVT belt had to get me all the way to Sydney, where I could pick up some more. Today, we were going to a tiny little place called Majors Creek to see my old mate Nigel Houston Begg. Majors Creek is a jewel nestled in wonderful country among the rolling hills behind Araluen Valley, where another friend had a place which would be our stop for the night.

I was excited about seeing Nigel. He's quite mad, a dedicated motorcycle man who eats, sleeps and breathes everything bike-related. He used to be a daredevil of sorts, once jumping a mountain bike over I can't remember how many buses—let's just say there were lots. That was back when mountain bikes were just regular bikes with slightly wider tyres. Over the course of his life he's had many passions; his current one is all about getting back to the basics. So some years ago he sold everything, purchased a large chunk of Majors Creek land onto which he put a 40-foot sea container full of motorcycles, and moved in. The container has no power or running water, in fact no amenities whatsoever, just Nigel and his bikes. I thought he had finally cracked back when he did it, but I was wrong: I've never seen him happier.

That could have a lot to do with the young lady from Belgium he rolled up to meet us with—on a tandem bicycle—outside the Majors Creek pub later that day. From there we followed him out to 'the container'. It was spectacular; Nigel had made it very comfortable. There was a creek running past the front door. Nigel pointed to a clump of bushes near it. 'There's our laundry,' he grinned. I got the tour of the inside. 'Feel the temperature drop when you walk in?' he asked, and I nodded. 'That's the nature of tin box.' He had a generator for power, a gas stove, everything you might need (on a basic kind of Nigel level).

We swapped a few stories, had a whisky and decided to go down the back road from Majors Creek to Araluen. I love that track; it's just a small dirt road but it's fast, steep and a lot of fun. Dan climbed on the back of Betty to film, and Eddie drove the truck round the long way to meet us at the Araluen pub.

'I've never been on the back of a bike before,' said Dan, looking a bit worried, more for the brand-new thirteen-thousand-dollar camera in his backpack than anything else.

'Don't worry, Danny, it's all downhill mate, just hang on,' I said. Nigel rode beside us. The track was a blast, Dan letting go with a few screams on some tight hairpins when I let the back wheel slide out near the edge, giving him time to look over and realise there was no railing, just a sheer drop a few hundred feet down a cliff.

We were on our third beer at the pub in Araluen when Eddie showed up.

After that it was on to Gail's place for the night. She was away in Sydney at the time, but being the legend she is, she'd left us a roast in the oven, apple pie in the fridge and cold beer in the esky. That night was like every night I've ever spent on that property, just brilliant. With a full belly and the peace and quiet, I slept like a baby.

In the morning Eddie got up early and fixed us a full cooked breakfast. Dan wanted to go for a ride to get some shots, so he jumped on the back of Betty again. We plodded through a few paddocks, cresting a big hill to pull up right in front of the biggest bull I've ever seen. He was magnificent. It looked like someone had stretched a hide over a drooling city bus. The big beast blew snot out of nostrils you could fit a fist in.

'OK mate, we've seen the giant bull, let's move on,' Dan said nervously.

The bull turned and started walking towards us.

'Pauli, let's go, c'mon mate,' Dan said.

I pulled off very slowly. Dan didn't think it was funny.

By lunchtime we were past Batemans Bay and heading for Kiama and a great night with another old friend of mine, Jane De La Vega.

About twenty k's out of Batemans Bay, I was going down a hill sitting on 90 when Betty's back wheel suddenly locked up. She bucked wildly, her back wheel sliding then freeing up again. I nearly came off. The idler sprocket, shaft and housing had sheared off, flying into the main sprocket and chewing everything to pieces. This was a big repair, not something I could do roadside. I needed a new chain, sprockets, shafts and bearings.

Betty went into the back of the truck for the third time. I sat there, worries filling my head. I had to get the bike to Matt Bromley in Sydney; once he'd worked his magic on it I could relax, and hopefully spend no more time sitting there on the back seat. We rolled into Jane's driveway two hours later, to be met by a great home-cooked meal, hot showers, and lots of good conversation.

The next day we got an early start for the last run into Sydney, another two hours down the highway. I called Matt at Deus; he was ready for us to bring Betty straight into the workshop. This whole leg had seen me relying on mates to get me through; sometimes friends make all the difference.

14 WALLET

Clare and Lola would be waiting for me in Sydney. My dad, who had flown all the way from the UK, would be there too. He was going to join Phil and Dan in the truck up to Brisbane on the next leg. The time I spend with my father is great now, though it hasn't always been that way. We were separated for a long time by my work and a lack of communication that lasted far too long. I was looking forward to seeing his face when he finally laid his eyes on my daughter for the first time.

I was a little apprehensive about getting the bike fixed, and having my family shacked up in a hotel while all this was going on. I would be busy every day helping Matt with the bike, plus I had to find spare parts, and I didn't have a clue how long all that was going to take.

Betty rolled into Matt's workshop on Thursday afternoon. I had Friday to find all the spares; on Saturday I had a racing suit fitting and Clare had to go to a funeral so Dad would have to look after his new granddaughter.

The racing suit fitting was important. Through Deus I had been put in touch with Rory, the Australian supplier of Gimoto racing leathers, world-class Italian-made racing suits. That gear is normally well out of my reach, however Rory had heard about the HPDM project for the Speed Week flying kilometre and very generously offered me a set of leathers for the salt. I was stunned. 'Mate, I think it's great,' said Rory when I called him. 'We love to get behind this kind of thing.' He was going to meet me at Deus on Saturday at noon, and Dan wanted to film the fitting for the show.

At Deus, Matty was as keen as ever. 'So, this is Betty,' he said, and he looked her over. 'Mate, if you're going to keep punishing yourself on this thing, we need to rebuild the whole sprocket and shaft system. How much time do you have?'

'Not much. Money's tight too.'

He sipped his coffee. 'Well, I'll get started. Don't worry, mate, we'll look after you. Now go and see your girls.'

A great sense of relief washed over me as I handed Betty over to Yoda. Fix it, he will.

The other two mechanics looked over the top of the bikes they were working on. 'Is that thing diesel?'

On the way out I stopped in the café for a brief moment with Eddie. His wife Katrina was there, so I got a chance to say thanks to them both. They're good people, the kind that make the world go round.

When I got to the hotel, Dad was already there with my girls. Everyone looked great. I had missed my father's first contact with the next generation, but life is like that. It didn't matter, I was just glad to see him there holding Lola, so very happy. I hadn't seen him in two years, but we picked up right where we left off. He would be with me for the next week, supporting me—he'd even brought the single malt.

I stayed at the hotel for an hour and then went back to help Matty. He had already stripped the shit out of the bike. 'OK, mate, we need to replace all that, but with bigger bearings and shafts. You're going to need the same sprockets but they need to fit round the bigger bearings.' He pointed to a box of stripped parts.

Taka was there too. He'd already ordered a new chain but the drive and idler sprockets were not off-the-shelf items as I had been told. 'No, not available off the shelf, I'm afraid.' He picked up the smashed idler sprocket and held a vernier to it. 'Custom size.' Taka may be as laid-back as it gets, but he still has that wonderful Japanese sense of precision and efficiency. He's probably on the ball even when he's asleep. I've got nothing but time for Taka.

I called Rob at the uni's workshop, and told him what we needed. 'Not a problem, mate,' he said. 'I'll courier the lot up to you today.' He would also make, from scratch, new shafts and sprockets all properly hardened and ready to go; however this would take four days, which meant that I'd get back on the road by next Thursday if I was lucky. My other problem was the CVT belts. In the three years since the uni built Betty, the firm that fabricated her CVT belts had gone out of business.

Rob couldn't believe I'd gone through the lot. 'You've got none left? I'll try looking from my end.'

I started ringing around every drive-belt supplier, importer and manufacturer in Australia. The belt had very specific parameters, as nothing on the bike could be moved to fit the belt—the belt had to fit the bike. I had some luck with CBC Bearings, and fixed a time to go out to their warehouse the next day. That evening was spent chatting to Dad, but by eight o'clock I was falling asleep, exhausted.

On Friday morning I had coffee with Matty at 7 a.m. He was busy with several other bikes, so Dan and I went out to CBC Bearings and met Steve Hudson, the Senior Applications Engineer, and the New South Wales General Manager Lou Amato. They listened as I described my problem, then walked me into a warehouse big enough to park two 707s.

On huge racks stretching to the ceiling were thousands of drive belts. 'Right, what size do you need?' asked Lou. I told him, and there was a moment of hope. I was standing there, surrounded by millions of drive belts;

surely there wasn't a drive belt on the planet that they didn't have. But guess what? They had drive belts that were close to my requirement but not exactly the one I needed.

I was stunned. They saw the look on my face. 'Don't worry, we'll get the right belts, Paul,' said Lou. Steve offered to come all the way across Sydney to Deus and have a look at the drive system on the bike. He couldn't believe that the belts we had access to would not work, so we drove back to Betty with a box of belts. Matty and I reassembled the bike and for the rest of the day we tried all the belts, one by one.

There was one that was almost the right size, and would work at a pinch. 'I can get a slightly smaller version of this belt in from Mexico in a week; it should work fine,' Steve said. He had saved the day. 'We have enough of these to get you going, and the rest can be sent on to meet you. Just let me know by phone where you are and I'll freight them to you.' Steve even sold me the belts and bearings to match the new shafts and sprockets at cost. I was stoked and mightily relieved.

Matty was getting ready to knock off for the weekend, and he handed me a beer. 'Mate, we're not coming in this weekend, but here's the key—you make yourself at home and use all my tools. With any luck we'll have the shaft sprockets on Tuesday, whack 'em in and you're off.'

That night I walked across the street to the hotel doing the maths in my head. I was rapidly going over my budget for spare parts, but there was no backing out now. All I could do was move forward. Tomorrow I would finish changing out the nuts and bolts on the bike, then pull the front end off the spare bike and fit it to Betty.

Saturday found me in the workshop at 6 a.m. with a coffee, the radio and more tools than I'd ever seen. Meantime in Adelaide, Rob had received via courier the parts we'd pulled off Betty, and he spent the weekend machining new sprockets and shafts. I continued pulling every nut and bolt off Betty and replacing them with high-tensile steel ones, nylock nuts and lots of thread lock. She had shaken herself to bits. The front end was a mess, the triple clamp was worn; the forks vibrating had taken its toll. Everything was stripped and replaced.

The morning passed quickly. At midday Rory called me to say he was waiting for me in the Deus café. I washed the grease off my hands and ran around to meet him. 'Can't thank you enough for this,' I said, and shook his hand.

'No worries, Paul.' Rory was very relaxed and easy to talk to. Dan arrived with the camera and set up in the middle of the shop, and Saturday afternoon shoppers and bike nuts milled around watching.

Rory had obviously done this kind of thing before. He talked easily to the camera, he spoke well and knew exactly what he was talking about. He described the ideal fit of a riding suit for professional racers and amateurs, and explained the difference from a rider's point of view in the different suit designs as well as different types of leather. 'Right Paul, if you could hold out your arms like so,' he said. I did as I was told, and Rory started taking my measurements, then entering them into his laptop. I was rather enjoying the whole thing, until Rory got to the crotch measurement. 'OK, Paul, I need to get the tape directly on the skin here, so I'll need you to hop out of your jeans.' There was a pause while my mind raced for an answer.

Rory grinned. 'You're not wearing underwear, are you?'

I shook my head. Dan looked up from the camera. 'Mate, who goes to a racing suit fitting jockless?'

I tried to look penitent. 'Sorry, guys. I've been on the road and just ran out of clean undies.'

Dan was laughing. 'There are many subtle refined stages in the cycle of a man's jocks on a roadie,' he said, adopting a declamatory stance, placing one foot on his tripod case and leaning forward with an elbow on his knee. Shoppers gathered closer to listen. 'Obviously, after the initial soiling your first step is to simply turn them inside out and soil the exterior; next, depending on any skid activity you can wear them back to front, or burn them and go straight to the final stage . . .' he gestured towards my crotch, 'where Paul is right now, the free ball.' Dan smiled in a knowing way.

'Deus will lend you a pair of shorts, mate,' said Rory, nodding towards the clothing section. I asked one of the guys working there, grabbed a pair and raced off to the change room and was back on my spot ready for Rory to stick a tape measure into my boys.

'All done.' He shook my hand, we traded business cards and that was it. Dan packed up his camera and was off to enjoy the rest of the weekend in his home town.

I changed back into my filthy jeans and went back to pulling the bike apart. By 4 p.m. I was getting tired. We were supposed to be heading out for dinner that evening with Dad. It had been very dull in the workshop without Matty to bounce off and learn from.

I called Clare to tell her I was shutting it down for the day. Dinner was booked for six so Lola could eat without passing out in her food. Just before I left I did the pat-down thing: watch, wallet, glasses, keys—no, wait, wallet . . . wallet . . . WALLET, WHERE'S MY FUCKIN WALLET?

A horrid pang of doubt ripped into my brain. I started a mad search around the workshop but found nothing. Panic started to fill me. Everything was in that wallet: all the funds for the trip on a Visa card, my personal cards, licence, all the usual suspects. I called Clare.

'Calm down,' she said. 'Now, when did you last see it?'

'When I got my coffee this morning.'

'Did you eat lunch?' she asked.

'No.'

'Honey, no wonder you get so tired, you can't keep skipping lunch. Right, start retracing your steps and call me back when you find it.'

I retraced them out into the shop a billion Saturday shopping punters had traipsed through. My heart sank. I bolted into the change room, but it wasn't there either. Perhaps the cash got lifted and they tossed the wallet? Eight bins and a dumpster later, I called Clare back. It was now 5 p.m. and dinner was in an hour.

'OK, sit down, have a glass of water and go over your day again slowly.'

I forced myself to stop racing and just sit. I thought hard about every step of my day. Then it hit me: when I'd got back to the workshop after meeting Rory, I pinched some chewing gum off Matty's desk, and went to the toilet. But the shop toilet was busy so I used the one in the workshop . . . so . . . I was the only one who's been in there all day! BANG—I slammed the toilet door open and was on all fours round the back under the plumbing quicker than a refugee in an airstrike, peering over half a dozen copies of *Just Bikes* and *The Picture*. There was no sign of it. I sat there on the floor of the toilet and thought about getting on the phone and cancelling everything. Was it too late already? Had all my accounts already been handivacked?

I stood up and stared into the stained porcelain. Fuck it, I had to check. I rolled up my sleeve and dived my hand in, right in, up to the elbow in, and had a bit of a gag when my chin nearly hit a yellow pee stain on the side and . . . wait a minute, my middle finger was touching the unmistakable corner of a credit-card-sized single-fold, polished black leather Dunhill wallet. 'YOU FUCKIN RIPPER!' A bent coat hanger finally got it out. I was so excited I called Clare immediately, toilet water still dripping down my arm.

'That's great, honey—where was it?'

'Oh, on the floor by the workbench,' I lied.

Having said all that I can assure you, had I not found my wallet, this book would still be in your hands now, but you would not know that I fisted a public toilet.

Dinner was a dismal affair in a nasty, cramped vegetarian restaurant. There were ten of us, we ordered, and an hour later I went for a walk with Lola who was getting very hungry and angry. We got two Subways and stood out the front eating them, then went back inside, waited for another fifteen minutes and finally gave up and went back to the hotel.

On Monday afternoon the bike was almost ready. All it needed now were the sprockets, shafts and new bearings. Matty had seriously beefed up the frame and brackets that made up the drive housing, he put on a set of highway pegs, and another set above the originals, so I had a choice of three different positions for my feet. All I could do now was wait. Rob's custom-made parts arrived on Wednesday afternoon and we put them straight in. I repacked the truck and got everyone organised for our departure the next morning.

15 STAGE THREE: LIFE CYCLE

On Thursday we were out the front of Deus, waiting to go. Dare, Taka, Ben and Matty had all come out for a chat. Again I had been saved by my mates.

Saying goodbye to Clare and Lola is never easy, but I pulled on my helmet, climbed on the bike, had one last look, gave a wave and we pulled off. My father-in-law, Phil, was driving the truck, Dad was in the passenger seat and Dan was in the back. Phil has driven trucks from Sydney to Brisbane for the better part of 30 years, so I just followed him out of town. Dan wanted to get a shot of the bike going over the Sydney Harbour Bridge, so we pulled over, stowed the doors, strapped him into the shooting seat in the back and made for the bridge.

Everything went well—well, almost everything. Betty's CVT drive fell apart, but that was because I'd forgotten to tighten up the bolts.

A massive dust storm had blown up from the desert the day before, sandblasting the city and turning everything orange. There was still a weird hue in the sky as we broke free of the traffic and headed north.

Stage three was a straight run up the Pacific Highway through Newcastle with a brief detour through Bucketts Way. It's a popular run for riders. Some parts of the road are not so great to ride on but at my speed and with all the vibration it didn't really make any difference. We meandered along with the Karuah River past wide paddocks and shaded forest, then turned left at Gloucester and on to Nabiac and the National Motorcycle Museum.

Our stop for the night was a small house in a paddock directly behind the museum. As usual we arrived late. Dad and Phil had spent the day on the road chatting and both looked tired, so Dan and I wandered over to the main entrance of the museum in the dark. A massive bike was displayed out the front. Dan lit up the camera, and its beam cut through the pitch-black interior, bouncing off hundreds of neatly lined up, polished handlebars. 'Wow.' It was an Aladdin's cave in there. I was like a drooling kid outside a toy store window at Christmas. I pushed on the door as if somehow by magic it would open and automatically all the lights would come on, beaming me through the looking glass and into Bike Nirvana.

The door of course remained locked, so I had to wait till morning, but as soon as the museum opened, I was there hopping about like a cartoon rabbit ready to spend my morning soaking up bikes, bikes, more bikes, bike stuff, bike trivia—bike everything. The place didn't disappoint. I have never seen so many bikes in one place. Imagine the *Titanic* was stacked entirely with bikes, that's how many bikes there were. Or you know those offshore firefighting vessels with their massive water cannons? Imagine they shot out liquid bike, that's how many bikes there were. My mind melted, I didn't know where to start. Every machine I'd ever wanted to take a gander at was there, but soon Phil and Dad were gently trying to wean me off the bike drip I'd so quickly become addicted to. 'Mate, we should think about heading off,' said Filthy.

'He's right son, let's go.' Dad had to drag me out of there to my own bike—my bio, no-power cement mixer of a bike. It was a bit of a comedown.

We continued on the Pacific Highway. Just outside Kempsey I shredded the last of the original CVT belts, so we put on the first of the new make-do ones I'd got from Steve in Sydney. Getting the bastard on proved to be a nightmare. An hour later we were back on our way to Grafton, where Clare has family. Her mum, Cathy—or as everyone calls her, 'The Cath'—grew up around Grafton. Filthy told me about Cathy's cousin, Don Walker—'Great songwriter,' he said. Over the years Mr Walker has penned an astonishing array of chart successes for the likes of Cold Chisel and others. 'You know the song "Flame Trees"?' asked Filthy as we entered Grafton.

'Mate, I love that song.'

'Well, that's about some trees here in Grafton,' he said. We stopped for a quick visit with the family and then continued on to Ballina, our stop for the night.

'There it is, mate.' Filthy's voice woke me; I had gone catatonic on the bike again.

'Where's what?'

'The Big Prawn,' he said. Yup, there it was, Ballina's pride and joy, looking a bit run-down and scary. Usually all the big things, like the Banana, the Pineapple and so on, are a bit polished, they look kind of soft and familiar to the eye, but the Prawn looked like a dirty alien and certainly didn't make me feel like diving into a big plate of prawns.

As it happened, it was time for dinner. 'I think I'll have steak,' I said. Later, my belly full and the beer icy cold, we sat around talking until my lids started to droop. A hot shower and a soft mattress beckoned.

By 8 a.m. the next day we had passed Mullumbimby, where my good mate Erwin has a property. Four years ago, Clare and I stayed there with Erwin and his wife Lucy. He's worth visiting just for a trip to his toilet; called 'The Long Drop', it's just a little outdoor dunny in a shed with no door, set right at the crest of a hill that gives you an amazing panoramic view down a valley. I was just sitting there, minding my own business, when yes, you guessed it, I did the 'Exposed-Arse Spider Dance'. This version differs from the others, but only in the most subtle ways; essentially it's just a flat-out sprint and roll.

By mid-morning we had crossed over into Queensland. By then we were back on the Pacific Highway and I was back to feeling silly each time a big, ballsy, hairy-armed biker sidled up for a look. As I sat in my upright bio-fuel typing-pool riding position, hairy-armed bikers glanced over at me with a mixture of pity and amusement. Seated astride their Harleys in that laid-back, reading-the-weekend-paper-in-the-armchair position they travel past me effortlessly, their bikes sounding like several howitzers going off in unison. Even when bankers, lawyers and brain surgeons skip a weekend shave, get up early, saunter into the garage and throw a leg over their Harley, they get that face on, that look-at-my-bad-arsed-substance face. When they go past me, I can practically hear what they're thinking: 'I'm cool today baby, but next to this thing I'm really cool. Hey, I think it's a diesel.' I knew that for the entire ride I was never going to bump into another twat riding an irrigation pump, I was never going to go fast enough for anyone to want to ride with me, unless I befriended a retired biker in a golf cart. I was never going to hear someone say, 'Hey, you have a slow bio-diesel Frankenstein special, so do I—let's be friends.'

Lunch in a gas station, a quick pee, then a final push into Brizzy, where we dropped Dan and Betty off at a hotel in the city. Filthy had to grab a cab to the airport, and the old man and I drove across town in the truck to spend the night with John Lloyd, an old Air Force flying mate of Dad's, and his wife Glenda. John's a great guy; I ran into him at the Brisbane Writers' Festival last year. He had me in stitches with stories about Dad, and told me lots of things I didn't know about him. John's memories of those days, long before I was born, were clear as a bell, and by the end of the night I started to look at my father in a new light, like a veil had been lifted. They were like two young blokes again, bouncing off each other, laughing. I hope Erwin and I will be like that in years to come.

16 STAGE FOUR: FOLLOW THE BLOOD-SPLATTERED BRICK ROAD

Mathew Downey, Clare's big brother, is not physically big—in fact, none of Clare's family is big. But what they lack in height they compensate for in character, and Matty is no exception. He was waiting for me with Betty and Dan in the city centre, his bag packed and the obligatory Downey silly hat parked on his head. We stood around outside his hotel for half an hour. I said my goodbyes to Dad, John and Glenda; Dad looked good standing there with his old flying mate. I was itching to get going. Soon Betty was shuddering away under my arse, the Sunday morning traffic was minimal, and we peeled off into the city, waving. I got lost a couple of times, eventually hitting the Warrego Highway en route to Toowoomba.

Truth be told, I was feeling a little shitty. A few riders I'd chatted to before Brisbane, including Howard, had told me about an amazing ride through Brisbane Forest Park to a place called Mount Glorious; apparently it's a world-class blat. Once they'd stopped laughing at Betty they all said the same thing: 'Don't bother on that thing, mate, come back and do it on a real bike next time.'

I tried not to think about it, but it was a still, gloriously sunny morning, and soon huge packs of Brisbane riders were swarming in my mirrors then shooting past me, *whap, whap, whap*. Dozens of big sports bikes vaporised into the distance doing three times my speed, no doubt on their way to Mount Glorious for coffee. If I lived there, that's what I'd have been doing that morning. A few riders, puzzled by my smoky slipstream, pulled up level with me on the highway, flipped up their visors, eyeballed Betty's shuddering frame—dry-humping me violently at 80 kilometres per hour in the slow lane— and at the top of their voices fired off the standard: 'Is that fuckin thing diesel, mate?'

My ride eventually went from 80 to zero. There's this giant hill outside Toowoomba and Betty didn't stand a chance. Back in the truck she went; this time I managed to get her up the ramp without stacking her. Even our truck struggled to get up that hill, doing the last few kilometres in first gear.

We stopped in Toowoomba for something to eat. Matty had a good laugh at just how slow Betty actually was, and asked whether I enjoyed the humiliation of all those riders zapping past at light speed. He wondered out loud if Betty was in fact not a motorcycle but rather a machine for destroying drive belts cunningly disguised as a bike. I took it all, knowing that Matt, a strict vegan, had his coming. We were approaching the outback— no place for a vegan. Sure enough, every time we got hungry, poor Matty went through the inevitable horror of trying to find something to eat. People just don't get vegans; I heard countless roadhouse employees rattle off what they could do for him, but, oh, that's got mayo in it, or ham, or egg—sorry mate, how about a bread roll? On the trip his standard meal three times a day was any fruit he could find, fresh or tinned, and a salad roll, and by that I mean a bread roll with no butter and two lettuce leaves, perhaps some tomato or cucumber if he was lucky. Failing that it was a bucket of hot chips for breakfast, lunch and dinner.

By Toowoomba, Betty had chewed through four of the interim CVT drive belts. We only had one left. We decided to take a punt and push on to Roma; I called Steve and asked for the belts coming from Mexico to be delivered out there. We pushed on. The new belts should be in Roma tomorrow, and fingers crossed, so should we.

I'm not sure where the outback begins and ends in Australia. We passed signs now and again telling us we had just arrived in the outback, but I preferred to gauge this based on when road signs started warning me about getting clobbered by kangaroos, cattle, sheep and camels—and let's not forget the local armed outback Queenslanders; I definitely knew I was in the outback when I saw signs peppered with bullet holes. That, and my body was slowly cooking. This was the first of our long, dry and painfully slow stages into the red heart of the country. Matt hung back about a kilometre behind me, occasionally giving me a heads-up via the radio on a fast-approaching road train. This gave me enough warning to stop the bike and get off the road. Without Matty's warnings, I would have been in trouble; with all the vibrations my mirrors were effectively useless. The alternative was a road train—a massive thing that looks like a building with wheels—barrelling up behind my back wheel doing 130 kph and with no intention of stopping. Even pulling over had to be done with great care, as the shoulder was soft, and littered with dry sun-bleached animal bones that could puncture a tyre.

Roma was the goal; Roma was a place to rest for the night. I focused on the road ahead, and forced myself to pay attention. You live inside your helmet on a long-distance ride, but it becomes Wally World after a while. You drift, way off into other times, other places. While I rode I made lists, thought about tits, planned extensions to my house. I thought about the past a lot, revisiting childhood streets and alleyways in Scotland, like a morbid Google Earth. I jumped forward and backward through my past, made lists of people I wanted to catch up with, then crossed off the ones who were dead.

The problem is, if you let your brain box wander, your bike will eventually follow, likely straight into an oncoming road train. Rule of thumb, as I was repeatedly told by mates who know, guys who are long-distance riders: expect the worst, plan for the worst, and know yourself before you go. I have spent long isolated times away overseas with only my mind for company, so I knew hour upon hour, day after day of riding alone with only my thoughts rattling around in that helmet would be OK. Sometimes it would be a little dark, perhaps a little sick, but always within the realms of sanity. And of course I knew there was a truck a few k's behind me, so no matter what, I had back-up. That made all the difference. Attempting a ride like this on Betty without back-up would have been foolish.

When we stopped to refuel and drink some water, Dan would hop out of the cab while I was filling up Betty and ask me questions with the camera rolling. The answers I gave him were not always decent, polite or civil, or even comprehensible. But he rolled anyway. It helped keep me sane.

I ran into other riders along the way, guys chucking The Big Lap like me. I tip my hat to all of them: they were out there alone. Some had gone bush, tackling the likes of the Gun Barrel Highway, the Canning Stock Route or Gibb River; some were just mad, having completed the Finke Desert Race—basically, about two hundred k's of old railroad service track through the bush from Alice Springs to the town of Finke. Not too bad, I hear you thinking, but this track is hell on earth; you would be safer thrashing your bike across a minefield. There are corrugations deep enough to park a car in, and there's no maintenance done on the track—ever. But that's OK because you're doing 140 kilometres an hour; at that speed you're just planing over the top of everything and hanging on for dear life. So I listened while Geoff, the rider I chatted to during a break in the town of Jackson, told me how the Finke nearly killed him. Then he turned his attention to my steed. 'Is that fuckin monstrosity a diesel?'

There are countless disadvantages to riding an experimental bike like Betty around Australia, lack of power being paramount. Close behind is the lack of comfort—the vibrations had my arms feeling like they had just come from the dentist; I kept dropping things— and at this point, the lack of spares. We were down to the last CVT belt, and Roma was about 80 k's away. I waved to Geoff and took off, praying to the god of spare parts that my drive belts would turn up safely in Roma, all the way from Mexico.

Soon after Jackson, the road up ahead changed colour. I call that colour 'Hint of Death'; it's not quite brown, more of a reddish-brown mix. If this stretch of highway on my map was scratch-'n-sniff, then most people would vomit when looking at it on the way through Queensland. Plus, it looked like I was about to cross the frontline into some kangaroo civil war; littering the road before me were hundreds of stinking smashed carcasses in various stages of decomposition, from just splattered to bleached skeletons. I could smell it before I could see it, that rotting stink. Everyone else on the road was moving fast enough to rip through the pong before it made them gag—for other riders sitting on 130 kph it was just a matter of picking your way through the carnage and missing a breath. For me it was half a dozen breath mints and a prayer to the CVT belt: 'Don't fail me now.'

Australia relies heavily on the humble truck, the road trains that snake through our major arteries, but they don't stop for anything, especially the wildlife. Some parts of the road resembled streets I'd seen in Kabul right after a bomb had gone off. There were bits of bodies all over the place, and with the bits come the birds. But here it's not the odd crow, it's packs of crows, big ones, and the formidable wedgetail eagle.

Those birds are masters at playing chicken, no pun intended. Many times during the ride I came around a corner to find a giant wedgetail enjoying the never-ending all-you-can-eat road-kill smorgasbord. They would have heard me coming a mile away but just sat there motionless in the middle of the road, giving me the 'one day soon' look before reluctantly moving off at the last second.

Our ride into Roma was very tiring; the sun had turned my helmet into a convection oven. Finally we reached the town, and Matty got on the GPS and navigated us to the motel.

Roma is where Australia's oilfield started; the first wells were drilled out here in the late 1800s. I knew there would be enough oilfield hands milling about to make the next 24 hours interesting.

We pulled in to the motel, truck first, at dusk. I hopped off Betty and tried to cross my numb fingers while I asked the motel manager if a courier bag had arrived for me. Nothing. I tried to fill in the registration card, but my dead hands couldn't form letters so Dan had to do it. The motel was laid out in a big U shape and we had to drive past all the rooms to get to our room for the night. The place was full of oilfield hands, who sat out the front drinking in small groups. They tracked our slow circle round the car park, pulled the standard squint at Betty and wandered over as I got off and slid my sweaty head from inside my baked helmet. 'Mate,' said a big fella sporting a roll-up that dangled from his bottom lip and a sauce-stained, hard-yacka work shirt. 'Is that fuckin thing diesel?'

We all chatted for almost an hour, swapping stories and drinking beer. Then I got on the phone to try to find out where the CVT belts were. Steve was as encouraging as ever. 'You'll have them tomorrow, mate, late afternoon.'

I hung up. Dan looked at me enquiringly. 'We're going to have to stay here for two nights, mate; the belts won't get here until tomorrow afternoon.'

Dan looked tearfully happy at the thought of a lie-in the next morning. 'I'm gonna get some beers,' he said, and took off. Matt departed in search of food he could actually eat.

I couldn't relax though. I had a routine, it had to play out every night, no matter how tired I was. The bike needed a going-over in preparation for the next day. I had a bad case of 'equipment anxiety'. I'm used to planning everything down to the last detail, but with Betty there were daily issues. Overcoming them was just part of the game played out each day. It was psychological warfare at times, a war of attrition between Betty and me. The wicked vibration from the diesel single shook lots of things loose, so I would lie there in the dirt with a spanner and cast my eye slowly over the bike, checking her from front to back. I had a little white paint pen to mark bolts so I could see if they had backed off. I changed her oil, cleaned her air filter, checked the fuel lines and oil filter. I checked the tyre pressure on both Betty and the truck, lubed up everything that moved and polished everything that didn't. Like many riders I have an obsessive compulsive

bond with my bikes. In Betty's case it was a pure love/
hate relationship.

Matt came back with Dan. They had bought a slab of
beer, two burgers with the lot and a salad roll. We settled
in for the night, talking to the drilling hands in the cool
night air well into the early hours.

Morning saw Matty putting a new sign on the back
of the truck; he'd been down to the hardware store in
town and come back with all the kit to make his own
contribution to the ride: 'Caution Slow Bike Ahead'.

He was standing on the porch with a coffee when
I came out to squint at the truck in the daylight. 'Nice
work, mate.'

Dan was still asleep; all that running around with a
big camera in the bush had taken its toll on him. 'Get the
fuck up, you lazy cunt.' Matty leaped onto the bed and
started jumping up and down until Dan got up.

After breakfast we decided to check out the Big Rig,
an outdoor museum of sorts dedicated to the history of
drilling in the area. We met the manager and got the full
tour, and ended up spending the whole day there talking
oilfield. Roma was very friendly to us, not just another
outback town but one with a rich oil industry background.
We pulled into the motel car park later that day. I ran in
to reception, and there on the countertop were my CVT
belts—all the way from Mexico. 'Yes!' I ran out waving
them at Dan and Matty. We could hit the road again at first
light. I was beaming as we rounded the car park.

This time some new faces milled about and there was a lot of laughter. A big bald Canadian guy sauntered up: 'Hey man, are you Paul Carter?'

I pulled off my helmet. 'Yeah.' I stuck out my hand, he shook it and started laughing.

'Dude, call your mom.' Everyone burst out laughing.

'You what?' Then the penny dropped. I'm not very good at staying in touch with my family; it's not unusual for a month to go by between phone calls to my mum. She lives in France in a tiny village—not that it makes any difference where she lives, she could live on another planet and still find me. I knew she didn't like the idea of me leaving my girls behind to go gallivanting around Australia on a motorcycle, and when Mum wants an update, she gets an update. She worked in the oilfield for 30 years and knows how to find people. I've been on rigs in really remote Third World toilets, where a two-way radio is considered top-notch, high-tech communications, and my mother has tracked me down.

This time she'd surpassed herself. 'G'day Paul, how's yer mum?' said the guy in the next room as we passed on the porch. I discovered that Mum had tracked my slow progress as far as Queensland and decided that Roma was an obvious place for us to stop for the night, so she got online and found the numbers for all the pubs and motels in Roma and simply started calling. It didn't take long for everyone in Roma to hear that the oilfield writer—and by all accounts, mummy's boy—Paul Carter hadn't called his mum for a month. Matty and Dan found all this hilarious. For the rest of the night as different guys knocked off work and returned to the motel, they each gave me a huge grin and asked how my mum was doing, and it went on for the next two days. 'Is that fuckin thing diesel—and have you called yer mother yet?' Finally I gave in and called her. 'Hi, Mum, I'm fine.'

The next morning Roma trailed off in the distance behind me: no more mum jokes, just a nice easy run on the Warrego Highway to Morven. I felt upbeat and well-rested. For people who don't know, riding a motorcycle for extended periods can be physically and mentally hard.

I heard a lot of shit before I left to go on this ride. I thought about that for a while as we slowly rolled towards central Queensland. There were many people who supported me, but there were also lots of punishers, the sort who stay safely within their comfort zones in suburban bliss and feel compelled to make comments like: 'Why would you bother to ride a bio-fuel bike round Australia? What's that going to prove?' or 'You girl, with your support truck' or 'You're not even going up to Cairns or off-road properly' or 'Mate, I've been round ten times . . . in the nude.' Several of them said, 'Your truck burns conventional diesel so what's the point?'

I would go through the motions of explaining that if I did convert the support truck to run on the same fuel as the bike then I would need to haul more fuel around than the truck could carry. You can't just pull up and get bio-fuel at every service station. Besides, I didn't have the funding to do all of that; I only had enough to cover the basics. Anyone who manages to tee up a big ride is doing well in my book, and I have huge respect for the adventurers who actually get off their arse and do it. In fact, none of the riders I met on the road made comments like that; there was only mutual understanding and curiosity about the ride ahead.

A few hours out of Roma, we pulled into a tiny smattering of buildings and a roadhouse. Matty filled up the truck and I parked across the street in the shade, quietly sitting on Betty. I began to take off my helmet when the ground started shaking and I heard the roar: dozens of Harleys rounded the corner; the riders braked and backed their bikes in next to me in a long row, back wheels to the kerb. Pulling off their helmets and gloves, they dismounted and slowly gathered around me and Betty. My backside puckered. They all looked like real bad-arse bikers, with full-sleeve tats, big greying beards and dark wraparound shades. Oh fuck, this is the bit where I get to find out if Betty fits up my arse, I thought.

'G'day mate,' said a particularly big biker with gold teeth and a black bandanna.

'Hey fellas.' I tried to sound confident, but to these guys I must have looked like a lost schoolgirl on a Vespa.

'Is that fuckin thing a diesel?'

Well, thank God for that, they were actually really nice guys. We had a good chat, then they all had a beer in the roadhouse and we continued on.

Matt came on the radio as we pulled out. 'Mate, I thought you were going to get proper fucked then,' he laughed.

'So did I, Matt.'

Next stop, Morven.

It took time to get from point A to point B each day, partly because Dan is a perfectionist. Several times a day the truck would speed up and overtake me, then Matt would pull over, and Dan would spring from the truck and set up his camera. When he was ready, I would ride past, so Dan could film me approaching and passing the camera. Then Dan would jump back in the truck, and Matt would start the process again. That, or Dan would get me to turn around and ride past again so he could shoot the bike riding off into the distance; this often involved having to do it a third time so Dan could shoot the ride with his long lens, or a fourth, fifth and sixth time because of light, weather, traffic, or some other problem.

Sometimes they would scout ahead looking for a good spot to shoot, and this was when a road train would usually come out of nowhere and scare the piss out of me. Sometimes we would pass something that Dan liked and both Matt and I would leave Dan by the side of the road or he would take off up a hill or into the bush with his camera, tripod and a two-way radio to set himself up for the shot. Then we would backtrack a few k's and sit there in the 45-degree heat slowly cooking, waiting for Dan's voice to tell us he was rolling. Once we'd ridden past, he would come over the radio saying, 'Shit, I didn't get the shot, do it again', 'Shit, there's a fuckin snake chasing me', 'Shit, my battery's dead', 'Shit I forgot the long lens', 'Where's my stills camera?' or 'Have you guys left me here? Come back . . . Hey, come on . . . this isn't funny.' Sometimes he took off into the bush and forgot the two-way radio altogether. This all added to my frustration; I had no idea how hard it is to do a ride like this on film.

Past two in the afternoon, we were heading into the sun, and the glare was directly in our eyes. I was riding with sunglasses, tinted goggles, and a tinted visor and I still struggled with the glare. We pulled into a dusty little place and stopped outside the pub, where I toe'd out Betty's kick stand and got off. A dozen or so young blokes were sitting under the verandah, knocking back beers and laughing. As I turned I realised they were laughing at me, but I nodded and smiled. One young man stood up, looking a bit pissed and sunburnt. He ambled over, puffing up his chest and grinning. Here we go, I thought.

'Is that piece of shit diesel?'

I smiled again—a bit thinly this time—and left my helmet on, just flipped up the visor. 'Yeah mate.'

He looked over my shoulder at Dan, climbing out of the truck with his camera. I turned around and thumbed the comms. 'Get back in the truck, lads, and go.'

'Are you fellas makin a porno?' the young lad asked. Interesting angle.

'No, why do you ask?'

'Well, you look like a big cock to me.' He had a laugh to himself, and his mates joined in.

'That's a coincidence,' I said casually. His brow furrowed, waiting for it. I glanced over at the boys sitting on the verandah; they were just pissed enough to go for it. Oh, well, I've come this far . . . 'Coz you look like a giant cunt to me.'

Game on. It didn't get that bad really; the bike was the first thing he went for, he missed on the first swing, and I was long gone.

Morven finally loomed up on the horizon ahead, being met by the sun on its way down. 'Let's go straight to the pub, I'm hanging for a beer.' Dan's voice over the radio sounded relieved.

We pulled up directly outside the small-town hotel and wandered in. I was pulling off my lid as I walked up to the bar; a middle-aged woman serving sized me up as I approached. 'Bald head, motorbike, you must be Paul.' I stopped, nodded. 'Call ya mum, there's a good lad.' She walked off. Dan was pissing himself and Matt handed me his phone.

We fell into our usual evening beer-swilling banter, and had a counter meal. Afterwards, I went through my ritual with Betty, and by the time I walked into our shared room wiping grease off my hands with a rag and talking to myself, the boys were already fast asleep.

The ride to Tambo the next day started with sore heads and no breakfast or coffee. Dan wanted to film the scenery, or 'go all Spielberg' as Matt said over the radio. It was just too hot and tiring to wait around, so I pushed off. The arid flat landscape went on and on. This was the first time I had strayed well beyond the truck and the radio's range; I felt weirdly free, like I'd been released. I wanted to go back and do the whole trip again, but alone, like a few of the riders I'd met along the way. I thought about Clare and Lola, and I wondered how Oswald was getting on; I hoped he was still alive. Then I thought, if he'd gone surely the cattery would have called me on the sat phone.

Last winter he walked up to the front door of our house and announced his intention to go to the toilet. He has kitty litter, but prefers to poop in the comfort of the front garden. So I got up and let him out, and then my mate Gavin Kelly dropped by. I was standing on our front porch drinking beer and chatting to him when Oswald had one of his absent moments right behind Gavin's heel. 'MMMMAWWWW,' yowled Ossy.

Gav jumped about two feet into the air. 'What the fuck's up with your cat?'

Oswald was sitting between the roses howling that late night, psychopathic howl: 'WHAT'S GOING ON WITH THESE GIANT ROSES? . . . WHAT AM I DOING HERE? . . . WHAT THE FUCK ARE YOU TWO LOOKING AT?'

'He's got cat dementia,' I explained to Gav.

'MMMMAWWWW.' Oswald started digging out huge scoops of earth. It had started raining, but that didn't bother him.

'Where's he going mate, China?' said Gav.

'Well, either that or he's remembered why he's digging a hole in the rain.'

'He's down to his shoulder there, how big does your cat shit?' Gav finished his beer. 'That's a bit optimistic, don't you think, Ossy?'

I shrugged. 'He's an oilfield cat, mate, he'll be running casing in that hole next.'

Gav smiled and we were about to walk off when Ossy suddenly puckered up and nutted one out about a foot away from his perfectly vertical hole. Then he turned around and filled in the hole, patting down the earth fastidiously. He sprinkled leaves over the top and everything. He turned to go and stopped dead in front of his turd.

'Fuckin hell.' Gav was in hysterics.

Ossy looked up at us as if to say, 'Now, how did that happen?' and sat there in the rain looking at his poop.

Clare came out onto the porch to get us. 'Come inside, guys. What are you two doing out here?'

Gav said the obvious: 'Watching your cat.'

Ossy followed us in, soaking wet. We sat down and got talking. After a while, our conversation was interrupted by Ossy. He'd passed out way too close to the gas heater and was now on fire, running through the living room screaming 'MMMMMMMMMMAAAAAAWWWWW.' He left a burnt-hair vapor trail down the hall.

'Jesus, the cat's on fire.' We put him out. Luckily only the top layer of hair was gone, and now so is the gas heater.

Back on the highway only static came back to me over the radio. Matty and Dan must be well behind me now, I thought. I put my feet up on the highway pegs Matt Bromley had installed, taking the vibrations off my knee to my back. Towards the end of the day a dust storm began brewing off to my left. There were flashes of lightning, and sudden violent wind gusts buffeted the bike. A huge willy-willy formed up ahead, spinning a curved cylinder of red earth into the brooding clouds. I was just happy not to be riding into the sun.

Every morning I calculated how far we had to travel that day, against my average speed, with a Dan ('Where's my . . .?') factor built in. I had become obsessed with watching the odometer ticking over: the first ton of the day was easy, before the sun got up there and cooked me. The rest of the day was agonisingly slow, the old mechanical wheel slowly rolling over. That afternoon, though, I knew I was less than twenty k's from town. Hopefully I'd get there before the storm got me.

'Paul, are you there?' Matty's voice crackled over the radio. The radio's range was good for two k's so they couldn't be too far away.

'Hi Matt,' I said.

'Mate, we'll see you soon in town, at the pub, over.'

'Roger that.' I thought longingly about a big steak dinner sitting on the countertop waiting for me with a cold beer.

Soon I was rolling down the town's main street. No one was about and the wind was hammering dust and tumbleweeds across the road. I parked Betty around the side of the pub and walked into the main bar; it looked very comfy inside and the locals gave me a smile. I could smell a roast. Ten minutes later Dan and Matty stumbled through the door.

'Dan's made an executive decision to get shit-faced tonight, mate.' Matt put his hat on the bar and rubbed his hands together.

The girl tending bar came over. 'Hi, guys, what would you like?'

'One Pale Ale, one Guinness, a whisky 'n soda, two steak dinners, and a salad roll no butter with chips please.' Matt smiled.

'She's hot,' said Dan, watching the girl walk off to put the order in with the kitchen. 'So's she.' Another young blonde walked past. 'And another—they're all hot.'

Not only did the manager have a very nice pub, he also assembled a bar staff entirely of cute backpackers. 'Watch and learn, gentlemen.' Dan put his camera on the bar and within five minutes two of the girls were flicking their hair while Danny was being cute and anecdotal.

'I guess they don't get too many TV cameramen through town.' Matt regarded the scene and then his salad roll and chips. 'Yummy.' He lifted the top off the roll and started laying chips down in a row. 'If I never see another shit salad roll . . .'

We had a ball that night. Dan was hammered and very, very funny. Matt and I spent the night talking to a local guy who spends the day removing all the dead animals from the road. There's that much carnage out there on the highway that a guy has to drive up and down it all day in a truck collecting bodies. Now there's a tough job. I sloped off and did my bike ritual before I got too pissed.

'Tomorrow we ride to Longreach,' Dan announced later in the bathroom while trying to brush his teeth.

The morning presented itself in white-hot blazing hangover napalm heat. Squinting and cursing, the boys dragged out their bags and loaded up the truck. Betty was good to go, all I needed was a new set of ear plugs to block out Betty's racket. Without the ear plugs I was deaf after an hour. Sometimes I stopped for a pee in the middle of nowhere in total, outback middle-of-the-day silence and my ears were still shattering the peace and quiet. The residual ringing would last for hours, drowning out a leading question from Dan, filming me while I tried to urinate in peace.

'Sorry?' I'd say, and he'd repeat it. Still couldn't hear it. 'Say again, mate?'

'YOU LOOK LIKE A DISGRUNTLED STORM TROOPER IN ALL THAT RIDING GEAR, HOW DOES IT FEEL?'

'WELL, IT FUCKIN STINKS DAN, COS IT'S 48 DEGREES OUT HERE TODAY, BY NOW IT'S ONLY THE STUBBORN UNDERSTAINS THAT'RE HOLDING THE WHOLE LOT TOGETHER. LOOK AT MY PEE—I DRANK A LITRE OF WATER THIS MORNING AND IT'S THE SAME COLOUR AS THE BIO-DIESEL.'

We needed a mental health day.

We did the usual ten retakes of me riding past a particularly interesting tree, while Dan, Matt and I hurled abuse at each other over the radio. Finally Longreach arrived. We had a fine meal, lots of water, and an early night.

17 THE LONG REACH

The heat radiated hard invisible waves, zapping my energy.
Today was going to be long; the truck was about one
k behind me, but Betty's hellish vibration distorted the
image in the mirror, turning one truck into four. No
matter what I tried, there was simply no conventional
vibration dampening system that would make a shred of
difference to the mirrors.

I flipped open my visor to wedge a Minty into my
mouth. The air was like a slap in the face—imagine
sitting in a sauna while someone holds a hairdryer an
inch from your eyes, that's what it was like. 'Fuck a
pig,' I often swore out loud, or I'd sing, or have long
conversations with myself like a mad person with
Tourettes. A corner came looming up with a triple
banking hard around it, always on the apex. You could

sit on the bike for hours on the straight with nothing and no one passing you, then the minute you hit a blind corner, a road train the size of Brussels would be coming directly at you. There was no time to react, other than just blindly hang on and hope for the best. Because of Betty's very upright riding position, the invisible wall of air displaced by a truck doing 130 k's would hit me hard. It was often like catching a sack of flour in the chest, while the bike got blown across the road.

I'd just got settled back in the saddle, the truck was in the right place behind me, my Minty was doing a fair job of removing the rotting road-kill smell and we were purring along at 90 k's, when the bucket of coffee the French woman made me that morning hit my bladder in a latte tsunami. The usual deal with stopping for a pee was to wait for a proper bay where I could take off the helmet and gloves, unplug the comms, and have a slash at my leisure and in relative safety. But this morning I told the boys over the radio to drive past me and keep going; I would just pull over, hop off, pee, hop back on again and catch up. No removing helmets and gloves; I just wanted to keep going. I checked my right mirror as the boys sped up and moved across to pass, Matt gesticulating mid-story while Dan pointed the camera out the window and angled his head into the viewfinder. As they drew parallel with me, I got off the throttle and slowly applied the brakes together as I pulled onto the dirt. The shoulder was as wide and flat as the road; it looked like it had recently been graded. Betty was about two metres off the road when she slammed to a complete stop.

Time and adrenalin put you in a weird place. I wonder if there is a word for those moments in your life when accidents happen: that out-of-body parallel universe you enter when you realise you're going to crash, just before you actually hit something. Time slows down; adrenalin transforms you from a disposable camera into a microscope.

The information I processed in those split seconds was astounding. If only I could make my brain perform like that all the time. For me, the initial horror—like the spike of a needle—then dissolved into calm hyper-awareness like I'd had a giant hit of Berocca. I was suddenly as calm and detached as at any quiet moment. As my head went through Betty's windshield, I noticed the odometer read five kilometres; I'd reset it when we left Longreach. 'Five k's,' I thought, 'that's not very far out of town for an ambulance to travel.' My body was thrown forward and to the left; I was obviously getting high-sided and was about to get slammed down on my left side, head first. I thought, 'It's OK, the airbag vest will go off now,' and then my mind flashed to an image of me throwing the vest on the back seat of the truck as we left the coffee shop not ten minutes earlier. 'Oh fuck.'

Thomas Mann said it well: 'We never really learn anything, we just become aware of things when the time and the potential in us coincide.'

I hit the ground.

There was a lot of ragdoll tumbling. The brain stopped processing, shut down and rebooted seconds later. I was looking through my visor at a very worried Matt; he was bent over me, slowly lifting the visor open. Warm air rushed in but I couldn't get any into my lungs. The impact had knocked the air from my body; I could feel my right leg and arm but nothing else. Usually when a rider stacks it, the normal reaction is to spring up instantly and stand the bike up. But I could not raise my head off the dirt. I suddenly felt very self-pitying. Visions of me throwing a ball to Lola from a wheelchair wandered through my mind like a stray dog. 'Now look what you've done to yourself.' My sanctimonious common sense spoke up at last. 'Fatigue, not paying attention: cry me a river, you hedonistic wanker.' Oh God, what the fuck have I done? I tried again to get up but nothing worked.

Matt put his hand on my shoulder. 'What are you doing, mate? Lie still, the ambulance is on its way—ten minutes, OK?' he said calmly.

I became aware of Dan next to me. I grabbed his hand and squeezed. 'Don't worry, mate.' He faked a smile. It was bizarre to see Dan at this angle without a camera pressed up against his eye. I was grateful the boys were there.

The ambulance crew arrived, named Mel and Kim, much to Matt's amusement, then a fire truck, then the police. They were all completely brilliant, and fast. Suddenly there was a tarp between my head and the baking sun, and I heard the bike being carried off. My helmet was removed and all my gear. It was a frenzy of well-trained people, all of them knowing exactly what to do, unlike me and Matt. Once the ambulance arrived, even Dan got straight back to work and picked up his camera. Then came the pain relief, a big green tube, and whooooo the fuck am I.

Longreach Hospital's emergency entrance soon loomed up, reflected upside down on the ceiling of the ambulance. I was engrossed in that detached feeling you get with shock and strong pain-relief meds. This was just a movie I'd been watching; I'd seen this bit a hundred times—the gurney passing through several big swinging doors and pulling up next to the machine that goes *ping*.

The doctor marched up and said something doctor-ish like: 'So we've had a bit of crash then.' The green tube was removed and just as fast as I got happy the reality came thudding straight back, accompanied by fear. I was terrified I'd done something to my spine. The doctor asked what happened, and both Matt and I launched into the story while Dan filmed in the background. Suddenly Dan stopped and raised his hand. 'Excuse me,' he said. Everyone stopped talking and looked over at him. 'I've got the whole thing on camera.'

'Really,' said the doctor.

'Yeah, total fluke.'

'Well, let's see it then.' The doctor, Matt, Mel and Kim, a nurse, and the dude in the corner who'd been mopping the floor all crammed their heads over Dan's shoulder to peer into the camera's little video playback screen. There was a unanimous sharp intake of breath through clenched teeth, then everyone looked over at me flat on my back. The machine that goes *ping* pinged.

Longreach Hospital, although abundantly stocked with hot-looking nurses and extremely friendly doctors, unfortunately has no big expensive imaging machines with which to look into the human body for damage. They do however have a radiologist, who wheeled me away to X-ray my entire body. I was then wheeled into a semi-circular room at the end of a long corridor, and a few hours later the doctor reappeared with the good news: I had not broken any bones, though I had cracked two ribs, and torn my rotator cup, a groin ligament and my favourite riding pants. 'So in many ways it would be easier and less painful if you had just sustained a straight fracture.' He smiled and flipped over his clipboard. 'You're going to be with us for a few days. You'll have to eat prunes because the pain medication can cause some constipation. We're also concerned about any internal damage you may have sustained, so for the moment, it's all about you moving your bowel, OK Mr Carter?'

I looked over at the hot nurse who had given me morphine about 30 minutes before the doctor arrived. I knew I was grinning like a fool. 'So I can't go anywhere till I poop?' She looked at her shoes.

'Well, yes,' said the doctor. 'Remember to try to move about. You're going to be in a great deal of pain tomorrow, so we've given you sufficient pain medication to help you deal with that, and you've been admitted as a private patient so you have the whole room to yourself. The boys tell me they're going to bring some DVDs back for you later.' I looked over the doctor's shoulder at Matt, who was nodding and blowing kisses. Dan was doing that thousand-yard worried stare into nothing, the one he pulls when he's forgotten something. *Wait for it, wait for it . . .*

'Mr Carter, are you OK with all that?'

Dan's going to do it. Any moment now, wait for it.

'Mr Carter.' The doctor raised his voice and snapped me back.

At the same moment Danny said, 'Where's my phone?'

Right on time, Danny.

'OK, doctor,' I said. He could have just finished telling me I was going to develop a third eye and webbed digits; I had gone to morphine heaven. Gone. That is, until it wore off.

There was no self-medicating for me; I had to wait for the hot nurse to squeak her way down the hall to my pain-filled concrete room and jab that vein.

I woke up suddenly in the middle of the night from a dry, open-mouthed, drug-induced dreamless sleep. For the first few seconds I thought I was in another random donga, back on the road. It was like waking up inside Tupperware, all memory of the fall blissfully blanked. Until I tried to move, that is. The pain I felt in that dark room was more intense than anything I'd ever experienced, and I've broken bones before. For a second my eyes saucered as searing, all-powerful pain stopped me from sitting up. I couldn't even reach the little call button thingy to get the nurse's attention. Panic shot up and down my spine for a second, so I just lay there in the dark and focused on my breathing. Then I heard her shoes. I think I squealed a little like a Japanese schoolgirl in a Hello Kitty store. Thank God, she heard me, she's a hot nurse on her way, she's a fuckin angel, a morphine angel ready to jump on my midnight morphine roundabout, all the way to breakfast. I pictured perfectly poached farm-fresh eggs on toast with bacon and real coffee.

Instead, as the fluorescent light blinked on I looked up at a different nurse, older and grimmer, Skeletor in a white dress, who promptly shoved a pill in my mouth the size of a breeze block, followed by a straw. She took my temperature—for a moment I thought it was going to be the baby way from the look in her eye—she checked my blood pressure, scribbled on the clipboard at the foot of the bed and marched out, flicking off the light with a curt 'Try to get some sleep.'

The morphine kicked in eventually; I could feel it creeping around in my head with a pillow, smothering the screams.

The morning arrived with a gentle voice and a wheeled table gliding across the floor, pulling up over my waist. 'Breakfast,' the voice said, and a finger pressed the button to raise the back half of my bed. Someone opened the curtains to another hot sunny Queensland day. I looked up to see a homely-looking middle-aged woman; she smiled and slid a plastic tray onto my table with various round plastic containers no doubt housing a feast. But no: there was cold toast, fruit, corn flakes and yes, a big bowl of prunes. The doctor had said I would feel worse today and he was right. I couldn't see it but there was definitely an invisible elephant sitting on my chest, I was sore and felt completely crippled. My muscles just didn't want to work, I had no power; I was in a blackout on the left side of my body from my shoulder to my toes.

The hot nurse appeared. I could make out her underwear through her whites when she crossed the big round windows. 'How are you today, Mr Carter?' I was conscious of the fact that I looked and smelled like a bum. 'Enjoying the prunes?' she asked. I watched her young professional disinfected veneer closely. Where are you hiding those pills? She crossed the room again to refill my water cup, and I automatically checked again for the VPL. It's not that I'm a complete perv or anything, it's just what men do. Cleavage has the same effect, like looking at the sun or pulling on that little bit of skin next to a fingernail; every shred of your body says, 'Don't do it,' but you just can't help yourself.

She took my blood pressure and temperature, and brought in a huge purple Zimmer frame with retractable wheels which she parked beside the bed on my stronger right side. 'When you're ready, Mr Carter, use this to get yourself to the shower, it's just outside the door to your room. The toilet is next door.' I smiled, and yes, finally, there it was, the magic pill. 'The doctor will be starting his rounds soon, he'll be here by the time you've finished breakfast.' With a big smile and a quick retucking of bed sheets, she turned on her heel and squeaked out of the room. I could hear some loony shouting down the hallway.

God, I wanted to shower, shave and hopefully shit, thereby getting my departure ticket. But to what, a bike that I couldn't ride? I needed a plan. I had to call Clare; it had been twelve hours since the crash and I knew the boys hadn't made the call. This was on Dan's request—he wanted to film it. It's the call I never wanted to make, to tell her I've dropped it, to tell her to come to Longreach with Lola. The thought of my girls pulled hard at my gut, the morphine helping to produce crystal-clear images of Clare holding Lola, their faces happy, full of love, big as the sky.

Dan and Matt arrived with junk food, DVDs and real coffee. Dan did an about-face and walked out again, clearly having forgotten something. Matt's stocky purposeful stride stopped level with my head; he knew the first thing I would ask and he beat me to it.

'The bike's OK, mate; the front end's a little bashed in, the bars and the left foot peg are bent, the mirrors, tail-light and rear indicators are broken, but the frame is sweet.' He sat down and took off his hat.

'Where is it?' I asked.

'One of the fireys dropped it off in a ute at the motel this morning. How are you feeling? How are the drugs workin'?'

On any given day, all I have to do is look at Mathew and I'll smile, but on morphine I was grinning widely.

'Good stuff morphine, you look pain-free. That nurse is cute, she washed your balls yet?' He reached into a plastic bag and produced half a dozen DVDs. 'Now, the choices were limited, mate, this is the best they had.' I picked up the pile and in the process shifted my bum three inches to the right, causing me to wince in pain.

Dan reappeared. 'Where's my tripod?'

Matt looked at him and placed his index finger against his pursed lips. 'Hmmmm.' His other hand burrowed wildly into the back of his pants. 'Well, it's not up my arse—have you had a good look in yours?'

Dan smiled and put his camera bag down in the corner. 'Mate, local ABC Radio want to come by tomorrow and do an interview, is that cool?' I nodded. 'OK, I'll set that up.'

Matt's DVD choices were good considering he got them in a petrol station. Hitchcock's classic *The Birds*, *Ghostbusters*, an old Sean Connery sci-fi movie from the eighties called *Outland* and, God love him, Ewan McGregor and Charley Boorman's *Long Way Round*— just what I wanted to see. I'd rather rub Deep Heat on my balls and staple my tongue to a burning building.

Dan handed me my phone. 'Thanks for waiting, mate, I'll just roll.'

I called Clare. I didn't want to tell her I was in a hospital, that I'd dropped the ball. So I lied, telling her we'd decided to stay a couple of extra days in Longreach. She saw through my lie in a second, though, even over the phone. She was straight onto me, and got all the facts. She wanted to fly up straightaway, but in the few days since we'd last talked my daughter had developed a bad inner-ear infection that had just ruptured her eardrum, so they were temporarily grounded. Clare talked to her brother for a while, then Matt handed the phone back to me. 'Honey, I'll see what flights are available and call you back,' she said.

'Have you had a shit yet?' Matt didn't look up from his newspaper as he asked.

'No,' I said.

He shook the paper so the TV guide fell into his lap. 'Pity, this place sucks.' He put his feet up on the end of my bed. 'When did you have your last shit then?' He turned a page.

'Yesterday morning.'

'Right, that's 24 hours; you'd better punch one out for the team, champ, or we're all going to Darwin to get you scanned.' He tossed the TV guide onto the bed.

'What?' I looked at him and threw it back.

'Dr Feelgood and Nurse Ratched said yesterday you need to drop one within 48 hours or you're flying to Darwin to have an MRI.'

'Really?' I didn't remember that.

'Pay attention, 007,' said Matt, getting up. 'Now get your arse out of bed, have a shower, eat another prune-fuckin-McMuffin and poop for Uncle Matty or I'll wait till you're drug-fucked, get that crazy old cunt from down the hall, take out his teeth and make Dan film him with your cock in his mouth.'

That galvanised me into action, though I waited until they were gone to get to it. It took me twenty minutes to get out of bed and on to the Zimmer frame thing; the 50 feet to the shower was agonising. Hot nurse's voice came at me through the door: 'Everything OK, Mr Carter?' I must have been in there too long. I prayed she wouldn't poke her head round the door and see my pale, pathetic Zimmer-frame shower scene. I'd been trying to reach the back of my legs, and of course I dropped the soap.

'Fine, everything's fine, no problem, be out soon.' I overdid it; now she probably thought I was wanking. I brushed the socks off my teeth, shaved, and spent the rest of the morning pushing my pain threshold.

Dan arrived in the afternoon with Miss ABC Radio, and filmed her interviewing me in a wheelchair on the grass in front of the hospital. That was the first time I saw Dan film with his free eye open. Usually Danny keeps the eye not peering through the lens clamped shut, but now his free eye was wide open and wandering all over the ABC Radio journalist's gentle curves and blonde hair. Dan can do a great job of capturing the moment on film while having a good perv at the same time.

Later that night, while waiting for Skeletor to pill me out, I could ignore Ewan and Charley no longer. I could see the DVD cover on the chair next to the bed, the two of them sitting on their BMWs looking like a million bucks. I thought about my one bike, smashed up and stowed in a motel car park, and my leaky ten-year-old second-hand ex-council support truck. And then there was my support crew. Matt, well, he wasn't into bikes, he was neither sporty nor fit-looking—although he used to bowl when he was an alcoholic—he wasn't into road trips, he hates people, and every time Dan put the camera on him he spouted the most vile, disturbing, stream-of-consciousness rant, albeit delivered with real venom and wit; stuff that would peel the enamel from your teeth, make the hair on the back of your neck stand on end, if you were weak, old, or mentally challenged, would fuck you up. Yep, that's my support team right there. I wondered if Ewan and Charley had a Matt on their team.

In the end, alert from too much sleep during the day and still waiting for Skeletor, I gave in to the white-toothed allure of Ewan and Charley. It would have been easier to ignore blood in my urine; I just had to see what they did. I really enjoyed it, but I couldn't finish it. Not to detract from Ewan and Charley's efforts—I was fascinated—but I flaked out about halfway through.

That's when I met Bill—at least, I think his name was Bill—the crazy old gentleman from down the hall. My room was dark and cold, with invisible monsters hiding under the bed; I slept still aware of the crazy man down the hall, I was locked in the cell next to Hannibal Lector ready to swallow my tongue. I started to stir. Something deep in my subconscious was pressing an alarm bell. I woke with that disturbing sensation that you're being watched. I forced my eyes open. His nose was two inches from mine; I caught his cabbage breath in the same dark instant. 'Whoa.' My head jerked back hard into the pillow.

The TV still flickering with Ewan and Charley backlit his wild grey hair and creased leathery skin; he was babbling insane gibberish at me, nonsensical crazy talk, right into my face: 'Do you know the human head weighs eight pounds? Do you know that bees and dogs can smell fear?' He looked maniacal.

'Fuck off,' I said. I was scared for two reasons: one, because for a second there I was looking around for Dan and Matt in case Bill had indeed just been gumming my penis on film; and two, because even though I was to discover that he was very old and considered harmless by everyone, if he'd wanted to, this frail old bastard could have seriously fucked with me.

The light blinked on overhead. 'Out, back to bed, mate.' I'd never been so relieved to see the grim face of Skeletor. She gently but firmly shouldered Bill around the bed and out of the room, rather like a sheep dog nudging a lamb out of harm's way. Hot nurse no doubt had to deal with Bill's loose misfiring bowel and cabbage-breath-delivered bullshit during the day, and Skeletor had the task of rounding him up at night. This was not to say Skeletor was a dog; she just looked bad in that light at that hour of the night, when a man was seriously in need of more drugs. Soon she came back and hooked me up with the good stuff, thank God, so my pulse rate calmed down and I settled back into the BMW duo's well-planned ride. I need to watch it again one day when I'm not on drugs.

After my morning prunes in prune sauce with a generous side of prunes, I hit the Zimmer for an hour, then the hospital physiotherapist came by. 'Lose that girl's frame, mate,' he said. In his early thirties, he was tall and had a good sense of humour, he reminded me of Southwell. The frame got pushed into the corner while I stood in the middle of the room with my weight on one foot. The green hospital PJs were about three sizes too big, I just hobbled there like a big bald leprechaun.

'Hold on to my arm, we're going for a walk.' It really hurt, but slowly, very slowly, it did get easier.

Afterwards, I was in bed watching Oprah give another lesson in the real use of power, while crazy old Bill shouted nonsense from his room down the corridor, when suddenly that 48-hour back order of prunes hit exit point. Time was going to be critical. I don't know if you've ever seen a sloth panic; I did once, it's a super slow motion event—their top speed is fourteen kilometres an hour. You know the poor animal thinks he's doing 100, he's pulling all the right faces, it's just that he's going well under half speed. Well, today I was doing about five and needing to do about 105. That morning I had gone from sporting oversized PJs to one of those green reverse gown things that leaves your butt horribly exposed to the elements. At the halfway mark I realised I needed the Zimmer, so I had to make a brief diversion to the other end of the room, wasting valuable time. Clenching wildly, I angled the giant Zimmer towards the nirvana of clean cold porcelain, my already naked buttocks heading directly for docking. The music for *2001: A Space Odyssey* began to ring in my ears.

I focused on holding the clench, my balloon knot under increasing pressure as I reversed through the spring-loaded saloon-style doors to the toilet. The loud internal blitzkrieg in my bowel caused me to yelp in fear. I backed up to the throne as fast as my hobbling would take me, my knees started to bend, angle of impact looked good, five seconds to touchdown, stand by, stand by. As I reached the point of no return, I was no longer able to support my body weight, and I had to let go of the Zimmer and hope that I landed well. The inside of my right knee touched plastic and I let go. There was a sudden jolt of pain, easily a ten on the pain scale, as my weight came down directly on the middle of the seat. Shock combined with joy, combined with the knowledge that this—provided no internal organs were about to see daylight—could be my ticket out of here. Hallelujah.

In the meantime, hot nurse's desk was only a few feet away from the toilet door. The violent rapid bowel movement I was desperately trying to do quietly could in fact be heard in the Qantas Museum two k's down the road. 'You OK, Mr Carter?' Oh fuck no, her head popped round the door.

My voice went up ten octaves. 'Close the door.'

I sat there shaking and twitching for five minutes, then realised the roll of toilet paper was a good five feet from my useless left arm. The big red call button was two feet from my nose. All I had to do was give up and hot nurse would come in and really give me something to write about.

I stretched for the toilet paper, struggling against the pain, but fell short by an inch. I looked around for something else to wipe with. If I didn't sort this out soon, hot nurse would be back. I even contemplated ripping the arm off my backless green robe.

I finally bridged the gap—the long reach in Longreach—between my right hand and the petal-soft, fluffy white roll by using the toilet brush I found behind me. I discovered that if I smacked the brush down on the roll to make the paper spool out and waved the bristly end in the air, I could wind layers of paper around it. I was triumphant! But I was sprung. Hot nurse's puzzled face appeared once more in the doorway; I sat there looking at her, clutching my fairy-floss stick of toilet paper. There was nothing to say, so we both went back to work.

Why does this happen to me? It's not like I want to write about shit, but I'm the guy who loses his arse. In public. At least Matt will be happy.

18 IT ONLY HURTS WHEN I LAUGH

We are ready to leave Longreach. It seems miraculous but in four days I've gone from the bed, to a wheelchair, to the Zimmer frame, to the sloth hobble. Each transition was drug-assisted but still horribly painful. The hospital said I could go if I wanted to, but suggested I stay for a few more days before getting in the truck.

'Being here is getting easier for you now, but don't get ahead of yourself, Paul.' The doctor moved to the window and looked out at our old truck parked in the car park below. 'Sitting in that thing on our outback roads isn't going to be pretty.'

He knew I was going anyway; every day I was pushing my body closer to getting in that truck.

'What you need is time—you're going to be sore for weeks,' he said, looking doubtful. I must have looked like he'd just asked me to push a kitten into a blender. He sighed. 'Make sure you stop regularly and move about. I've organised some pain relief medication for you to use over the next two days till you get to Darwin. You need to sign for it, though.'

I hobbled over to him and he shook my hand slowly. 'You shouldn't go near that bike of yours for at least a month,' he said.

I smiled at him and hobbled off down the hall.

I could have hobbled onto a flight home, and spent the next month healing; the doctor and my body were both telling me I wasn't ready yet. But I was out of time and budget and full of pride and ego; there was no plan B, no backing out. The next 2248 kilometres to Darwin would be the fourth and last time the bike would be in the back of the truck, totalling 2427 k's travelled with the bike in the truck.

'The cherry picker can't lift a Jag,' yelled Bill as I passed his room. And goodbye to you too, Bill.

The elevator had a mesh folding door, the old-fashioned kind that you needed to close yourself. It took me five minutes to close it, and I was covered in sweat. I was as weak as a kitten, but somehow I had to climb into the truck and sit there for three days, so we could reach Darwin. I thought about the ride beyond Darwin. We weren't even halfway, we were just stuck in the middle of nowhere. I had to get to Darwin, get the bike repaired and repair myself, had to keep to some kind of schedule. Already we were two weeks behind and I was well over my budget. I had to push on. I'd found an excellent physiotherapist in Darwin who was willing to do nothing but work on me for a week, so at least that was organised.

To fix Betty, Matt Bromley, God bless him, had squared me away with a mate who ran a motorcycle dealership and workshop in Darwin. I could fly Clare and Lola up there to be with me for the week as well. I focused on that while I climbed into the cab; the seatbelt felt like it was made of lead. Lola's ear was on the mend; Clare had said on the phone the night before that she was taking her back to the doctor today for a check-up and hopefully an all-clear for the little one to get on a plane.

Heading out of Longreach, we stopped at that same coffee shop that we were in before the accident. I had another bucket of latte, and it hit my bladder at almost exactly the same place where I had dropped the bike four days ago. Matt slowed down as we passed the spot.

'We should do a piece to camera here,' Dan said from the back seat.

'Keep going,' I said. I didn't want to stand there looking at it. Matt nodded and got back on the throttle and back into the story he was telling.

Dan didn't say anything; he was very tolerant of

me, even though I knew he would be worried about the lack of footage now that we were all in the truck. Poor Dan was now stuck in the back seat with his small mountain of camera gear. The back seat was shocking: you couldn't hear anything over the engine noise, and the air-conditioning, which was barely enough in the front seat to lower the temp a few degrees, was just about nonexistent in the back. He was also sitting on top of the engine, and that barbecued your backside after the first hour.

Soon, however, I wasn't thinking about Dan's comfort anymore. By the time Matt pulled into Winton, 180 k's later, I was in agony.

Queensland's crappy outback roads would throw the truck's cab into the air every few minutes; my arse would leave the seat and come down hard, shooting waves of pain up and down my chest and shoulder. Because I could make out the potholes and bigger undulations up ahead I started tensing up and holding my breath just prior to the jolt, but this just made it worse.

As we pulled out of Winton the wheel directly under my side of the cab slammed into a bottomless pothole and I lost it. The next 2068 k's was feeling more like 10,000, and I still had over 8000 k's to ride after Darwin—that is, if I could ride after Darwin at all. It was a dummy spit to end all dummy spits, but it made me feel a bit better. After all, there was no other option, we just had to keep going.

During this nightmare of a drive, Matt was my source of light. Even at times like this he could make me laugh so hard I cried. His rants go way beyond my toilet humour and into a place that you reserve for the wrong stuff that on rare occasions pops into your head and leaves you wondering if you're actually mental and just don't know it yet. And because Matt's stories are so out there, Dan couldn't even think of filming us, much to his increasing annoyance. Matt would start out fairly fast and loose into his story or whatever he was talking about, enough to completely sucker you in; then he unleashes the Matt you didn't see, the one hiding under his mild exterior, the Matt that I call Bad Matt. Dan would throw himself back into the rear of the truck's boiling cab with his camera in his lap. 'Right, well, thanks for that, I can't use any of it.'

The Matt rant could occasionally get scary in the cab of a truck doing 130 kilometres an hour. At one point while spouting a story about anal sex, he was looking straight at me, gesticultaing with both hands off the steering wheel: he was so entertaining I almost got comfortable, until a pothole threatened to re-crack my ribs.

My morphine reserve was helping. Around the halfway mark, I opted to lie down flat on the back seat, and the magic pills put me away. I was in limbo, when the truck suddenly stopped.

I heard Matt talking to someone and slowly sat

up. There, in the absolute middle of nowhere, at an anonymous crossroads in central Queensland, was a group of eight lost backpackers. I got out of the cab; the drugs had me in their grip, and I wandered about on the baking hot road without a hat, looking at this group of carefree young backpackers. I don't remember where they were going, but one of them, a Canadian dude with a goatee, crazy hair and an eye patch, was playing a piano accordion.

My head was light as a feather, and Matt started dancing about in the middle of the road while Dan seized the opportunity to get some filming done. We all joined in. It was totally bizarre and very surreal, dancing a jig with the backpackers in the middle of the road in the blinding heat. Only in Australia.

The Canadian stopped playing, and his keen young eye spotted me as the one on drugs. He walked up smiling, with his eye patch and hair all over the place. 'Got some for me, man? I'm Carl.'

'Sorry brother, I'm a drug pig. It's morphine, I've been in an accident.'

'Oh, too bad, are you going to be OK?' He flipped up his eye patch and looked me up and down. 'Hey,' his finger came up and pointed at me, 'I know you, man.' I still had that feeling that perhaps I was still asleep and none of this was happening at all. 'Did you write that book about the rigs?' he asked.

'Yup.'

'No fuckin way. Wait here.' He bolted, and I turned to see him open the boot of their van and hurl all manner of crap into the road.

'What's the seal basher doing?' Matt walked up.

'I think he's got a copy of one of my books in that van.'

'Bullshit.' Matt threw his head back and laughed. 'Way the fuck out here. You serendipitous bastard.'

The young Canadian came bounding back with a yellowing, dog-eared copy of my first book. He'd hauled it all the way round the world to get it to exactly this point, where drug-fucked author met drug-fucked reader, at a crossroads in the middle of nowhere in the Australian outback.

I fumbled with the pen, tried to focus and wrote something profound and purposeful, the most encouraging, thoughtful, indeed inspirational thing I could think of at the time, a golden nugget of truth. Here's this guy, all of 22 or 23 years old, out on his first big adventure, eyeballing me and grinning like I'm a naked prom queen handing out free pot at a beer convention.

I have a responsibility to make this count, I thought to myself. I slapped the book shut and made him promise not to look until we had disappeared into the heat haze in the opposite direction. 'OK,' he said, and pushed the book into his pocket. We all shook hands and parted company.

I swallowed another pill and dragged myself into the back of the truck. Matt picked up right where he left off in whatever story he was telling as he pulled off the side of the road and headed towards Darwin.

'What did you write in his book, mate?' Dan was leaning over the front seat, his bearded face rocking from side to side with the truck.

'Dear Craig, avoid the clap, love Paul.'

Dan's face disappeared, leaving me dreamily gazing at the truck's roof, the hundreds of tiny dots in the fabric which gradually merged into blank sweaty sleep.

Mount Isa came and went. I know I spent the night there, I remember staggering out of the truck in the dark, in pain, and falling in a heap. I remember calling Pia, a friend who works in Tennant Creek, to tell her we would be there the next day. I remember Matty helping me back into the truck in the dark, in pain, the next morning. More pills please, Mr Brown Paper Bag from the Longreach Hospital. I don't remember crossing the border into the Northern Territory, but I do remember pulling into Tennant Creek. There I had a brief interlude of clarity.

We parked outside the first pub, as Matty always does, walked in and sat down. Within five minutes Dan nearly got into a fight with a bloke over his camera. Then Pia arrived; she hadn't changed a bit, she was full of life. We proceeded to get drunk, which of course is a really sensible course of action when you're full of morphine. While I was staggering about in the beer garden—well, more of a dusty shambles than a beer garden—Matt Bromley called to tell me he was leaving Deus.

'Oh shit, mate, what's going on?' I asked.

He told me he'd been offered a job on the team of mechanics hand-picked to build the bikes for the upcoming *Mad Max 4* movie. I could hear how excited he was over the phone.

'You lucky fucker,' I said.

'You're pissed, aren't ya.'

'Yup.'

'How ya feelin?'

'Well, put it this way, I'm not in any pain right now, brother.'

We bullshitted for ages. Matt was so happy; I was happy for him, he deserved it. Damn right. I wandered back into the main bar. Pia, Matty, Dan and another ten people were sitting there drinking and talking. My head was full of nonsense and morphine. I couldn't really join in; all I could do was listen and smile. Drinking in the Territory is like a professional sport; men seriously hit the piss there. Finally, we opted to bow out of the booze fest and get a pizza across the road. I waited in the outdoor dining area out the front with a bottle of water. Pia, Matt, Dan, a woman we found out was the drummer from the band The Go-Betweens, and another guy were all standing about chatting. By that stage I'd lost the power of speech and basic hand-eye coordination, but hey, I was in no pain.

The pizza arrived, and we were about to dig in when a car full of Aboriginal guys rolled up. A moment later another car full of Aboriginal guys rolled up. Everyone looked at each other. I know I looked like a wasted new graduate from some Nazi deportment school, so I hoped no one was looking at me. One guy from the first car asked where the guys from the second car were from. The answer came back—apparently from somewhere near Alice Springs. 'Well, fuck off back there then.'

The less aggressive second-car guys were outnumbered two to one. They took one look at us, pizza triangles dangling in front of our open mouths, and said, 'Hey, don't carry on in front of the white people.' All I remember was this huge booming voice from the first car right behind me. 'W-W-W-WHITE PEOPLE, FUCK WHITE PEOPLE.' The fence came down; it was on. I grabbed two slices of pizza and crawled under the table. Within a minute the pizza shop owner was out trying to separate them, and in another minute the police turned up.

'You right there, mate?' Dan was peering under the table at me, but my mouth was full so I couldn't answer.

The drummer from The Go-Betweens got me out from under the table and into her car. She dropped me off at the motel. 'What are you on?' she asked. I told her. 'Hmm, better stay in tonight then.'

Matty woke me up at 5 a.m. and we stumbled out to the truck. Dan fished out the last of the morphine from the hospital bag. 'Thousand k's today mate, all the way to Darwin. You're going to need these, that's the last of them.'

I pulled my sore arse into the truck. In the early hours, with no drugs coursing through my system, it felt like someone had been going at me with a baseball bat. Matt drove flat out, only stopping for fuel and hot chips. We drove into a miserable-looking, one-camel town somewhere before Katherine. I slowly sat up.

'It's weird here.' Dan was looking over to our left; there was a dust storm going full tilt outside, and everything was the same shade of light brown. There wasn't a soul to be seen, no cars, no signs of life.

We slowly made our way down the main street, and pulled into a service station. Matt hopped out, shielding his face with his hand against the sandblasting, and ran around to fill up the truck.

'Pump's not on.'

I staggered out and we ran over to the main entrance, rather like people do when they're caught in the rain, and stumbled through the open door. No one was there. We called out, but no one appeared. All you could hear was the wind howling outside. Dan came in, looking as perplexed as us. He shut the door, grabbed some bottled water from the fridge and plonked the bottles down on the dusty countertop.

'Hello,' Matt shouted. 'Anyone here?' We all leaned across the counter together to get a look into the back room around to the right. The door leading from there out to the back was banging against the frame in the wind, letting in intermittent plumes of dust.

For five minutes we just stood there, the wind flipping the pages of magazines on the shelf behind the counter like a team of invisible speed readers. 'You know, this is a bit like an Aussie horror movie,' said Matt. '*Wolf Creek* meets the Griswolds.' Dan was hooking into an ice cream, and I opened a bag of salt and vinegar chips.

'Actually, more like a zombie movie,' Matt said slowly, peering out into the street. We moved over to the window next to him, Dan with a face full of ice cream and me munching on more chips than one would consider polite to stuff into your mouth.

At first I saw nothing in the billowing dust, but then I noticed movement in the bush across the road. A figure moving forward, not in a normal fashion; they were doing a stop-start shuffle, arms a bit too rigid. 'Fuck,' said Dan, and stopped eating. So did I.

'There's another one.' Matt had his face pressed up against the window, trying to see through the dust and random airborne debris. Sure enough, another figure appeared, also moving towards the service station.

Maybe it was the previous night's drinking session, maybe it was the morphine, maybe it was just three overactive imaginations. Or maybe it was real; given the way my life had panned out up to that point, I could accept anything.

Dan let go with a nervous laugh. 'This isn't happening,' he said, and started to back away from the glass. 'Morphine or no morphine, they are not zombies, and this town is not deserted and I am definitely imagining all this,' I said.

Matt looked really excited. 'I hope they are zombies,' he said, eyeing a tyre iron by the fridge.

'AARGH.' Our heads snapped back to the window. The first figure was now passing our truck, still stumbling, hands outstretched; we could now see its face, covered in blood.

'Zombies.' Matt was up on the balls of his feet, as if realising this situation was ridiculous but ready to do something anyway. Dan's ice cream had melted down his hand, making a mess on the floor; he looked like a gay-porn-movie fluffer. I just stood there, waiting for an adult to come in and tell me what to do. We were all frozen to the spot.

The first zombie, a middle-aged woman in a ripped blue dress, pushed the door open, walked up to the empty counter and demanded a pack of Winfield Red cigarettes. At the same time a young guy came running through the back door. 'Bloody weather.' He stopped at the counter and took in the scene. Three out-of-towners obviously on drugs, and a zombie.

'WINNIE RED,' said the zombie.

'OK, OK, keep your hair on. You've been fighting again?'

The zombie ignored this. 'WINNIE RED.'

The guy put the pack down on the counter. The zombie opened its mouth, stuck its thumb and forefinger in up to the knuckle, and produced a gooey blood-soaked ten-dollar bill and some change.

'I've told you before about this, we don't accept money that's been in your body,' said the service station guy.

The zombie snatched up the packet quick as a flash and stumbled out.

'Any fuel, fellas?' asked the service station guy, switching his attention to us. He looked at Dan. 'Something wrong with the ice cream, mate?' he asked pointedly.

Dan snapped back to attention. 'Oh, sorry.'

'No worries, I'll clean that up,' the servo guy said.

'We need diesel on pump four.' I smiled, and went out to fill up the truck.

As we drove out of town Matt laughed for a full ten minutes. Every now and again I'd hear 'WINNIE RED' and he'd start laughing again. We stopped again in zombie-free Adelaide River for chips and diesel, finally arriving in Darwin in the late afternoon.

Matty had done a sterling job: he'd driven 1000 k's in one day, evaded zombies, done Dan's head in, and successfully taken the non-stop piss out of me the whole time.

I was so happy to see Clare and Lola, who were waiting for us at the hotel. I couldn't hug Lola enough. It was a good hotel too, the Holiday Inn, not a sweaty donga, or a flea-bitten motel room with stained carpet. This place had stars after its name. There are two Holiday Inns in Darwin, right next door to each other; Matty and Dan were in the same one as us, and Gavin Kelly, incoming support-truck driver and steadfast Scotsman, was flying in the next day and would be staying in the one next door. I spent the first night telling Clare all about the trip from Sydney while trying to ignore the pain that was slowly creeping back as the morphine left my system. But that night the pain was persistent and I had trouble sleeping. I concentrated on making it through the night. Tomorrow was a new day in the Top End, and would bring a 9 a.m. appointment with the physiotherapist.

It took me half an hour to hobble the two blocks from the hotel to the physiotherapist's office, Darwin's heat and humidity already making me sweat. I sat there in the waiting room, and waited. I picked up a five-year-old copy of *National Geographic* and pretended to read, but I was too nervous: this session was going to hurt, no question. A door opened down the hall, and the receptionist swivelled her head to look, turned to me, made eye contact: this was it. 'Mr Carter, you can go through now.' I faked a smile and slowly stood up. Rounding the corner I nearly bumped into the physio.

'Hi, my name's James, come through.'

I hobbled in behind him and he gestured towards a seat next to his desk.

'OK, you've asked for five days of physiotherapy following a motorcycle crash in Longreach about a week ago.' He flicked through some notes and looked me in the eye. A clean-cut guy in his mid twenties, he seemed well briefed and genuinely concerned. 'Did you bring your X-rays from the hospital?' I had them with me on disc.

After taking a good look he asked me to stand up and strip. I told him where it hurt, turned my head here and there, bent my arm up and down, did the hokey pokey and turned around, got on the bed and put my face in the hole. So far, so good: he was very thorough and explained what was going on in my body.

'OK, James, when can I get back on the bike?' I asked.

'That's hard to say. If you stick with the swimming exercises I outlined, we'll see how you are in a few days.'

'So when's it going to hurt?' I asked.

'Now,' he said, and pressed down on my shoulder.

At first impression he was all about a warm hand-shake, but this turned into a cold kick in the balls for the next hour. 'You do have a high pain threshold,' James said happily, making my leg fit into my ear while I spat phlegm at the ceiling and slapped my hand down on the vinyl. I know I piss and moan a lot; it's one of my coping mechanisms.

The next three visits to James—or The Painmonger as I came to call him—were intense. But the guy was good, and every time I left his office I felt better.

I said goodbye to Matty on the second day; he was flying back to Sydney and work. I was really going to miss having him around. On the same day I called Matt Bromley's recommended bike workshop, Precision Motorcycles in Berrimah. Matt had already phoned to let them know I was inbound, and he'd given them a rundown on Betty's particular needs. Tim Walker couldn't have been more helpful.

We got the truck over to them straightaway and I watched the workshop guys unload Betty. That was the first time since the accident I'd had a chance to look at her properly; the crash had done a fair bit of damage. The workshop manager, Darren, was straight onto it. Next the truck went in for a service.

At this point I didn't know if a week was going to be enough time for my 40-year-old body to climb back on Betty, or indeed if Betty was going to make it. One thing was certain: my funding had all been used up. Clare didn't know it yet but I was hacking into our savings now.

I found Gav poolside, sucking on a beer. He had flown his wife Jhovana and daughter Leonie up to Darwin to spend a few days with him before we left—that is, if we left. Leonie is an uber-cute, ridiculously polite eight-year-old; she loved playing with Lola. Clare and I loved that she loved playing with Lola, because it meant for a few hours each day we could sit in peace without taking endless turns at putting a stop to Hurricane Lola's vandalism. Jhovana is in many ways the perfect match for Gav: she's got the same wicked sense of humour, the same can-do attitude; like him, she can deal with anyone and any situation. I think it's got a lot to do with being an oilfield wife. But unlike Gav she doesn't possess the fast-food eating skills of a golden retriever, nor is she capable of sniffing out cold beer where there's no cold beer to be found; Gav could put a cold beer in your hand if he was locked in a bank vault. But they're lucky, because when you see them together it is obvious that this tall, tanned leggy brunette and the hairy, burger-necking, beer-sniffing oilman were made for one another.

'May as well make the most of the time here,' Gav said, raising his bottle at me. Gav is the original workaholic, he puts in massive hours, rig-hopping all over the place. This was the first time I'd seen him relax properly; generally he has a phone pressed against his ear. We'd usually plan to do something on a weekend, but then the phone would ring, and within a few hours Gav would have his head shoved up a tool joint in some oilfield pipe yard.

Together we explored the town as far as my groin would let me. I'd heard all the disparaging NT—'Not Today'—comments, but Darwin is actually a lot of fun and feels like it would be a relaxed, balmy kind of place to live. Every day could be a Sunday; every night could be Saturday night. It's packed with good-looking young people, packed like a Melbourne tram in rush hour during Fashion Week. There are manicured avenues lined with chic apartment buildings, and developments all over the place.

Every morning, I'd hobble to my physiotherapy appointment down streets sparking to life, past cafés frothing milk, and tourists looking for crocs. Every day the hobble back got closer to a walk, and every day my pain backed off a little more and my mood improved. By the end of the week I was feeling confident, and it was almost a pain-free stroll back to the hotel. I was dishing out my smiles to strangers and my change to the bums.

That night we went out on the town; the girls bailed after dinner, sensing the evening was headed for a boys-drinking-their-body-weight session. Gav and I bar-hopped about, looking for a place that suited us.

First was a slick, overdone, neon open-plan place that reeked of air-conditioned people under twenty. After that came a series of bars that just blurred together, ending in your standard every-Western-country-on-the-fockin-planet-has-one Instant Ye Olde Irish Fockin Pub, your very own slice of the Emerald Isle. Is there a factory somewhere punching out all the old Guinness signs and fake memorabilia? But the place was alive, the music was good, the beer was cold, and to Gavin's delight you could smoke inside without a bouncer dragging you out and shooting you in the head.

Donald Millar, the man originally slated to get me to Darwin, called us while we were at the pub. Gav waved his phone at me, yelling, 'It's Millar time.' Donald had just arrived in Darwin on his way out to his rig. While we had been on the road, every time we turned on the telly the news was all about the West Atlas rig. Donald was in fine form as usual, though he'd been through a lot in the past month. He sat down and gave us the whole story. With a 6 a.m. chopper booking he didn't jump into the beer pool with us; instead we made plans to catch up in Perth after it was all done and dusted.

I've never known a man to put in the kind of hours he did over the next few months trying to kill that well, and he was truly shattered when he lost his rig to an ignition and fireball that completely destroyed her. He took it hard, feeling deeply the impact of losing the rig, as well as the impact it would have on the ocean, the life in it and around it. All of this weighed heavily on his mind, you could see it in his eyes. His ability to bounce back is remarkable, and I'm proud to be his friend.

The next day we got the call that Betty was almost ready and the truck was serviced, so Dan and I grabbed a cab out to pick up the truck and then went straight over to check out Betty. We ended up spending the whole day out there; we replaced the tyres, tubes, brakes, bars, levers, tank, front guard, rear brake line, chain, sprockets and CVT belt; we welded the pegs back on, changed the filters, lines and injectors, and refuelled her. Finally she was ready. There was nothing else to do but get back on.

This was the moment of truth. Almost two weeks had passed since the accident. I slowly dragged my leg over the bike, the torn muscles firing bolts of sharp pain into my spine. I put all my weight onto the seat and started her up. She coughed, rattled for a while and began ticking over, *catonk*, *catonk*, *catonk*, sounding like she was chewing a steel mint.

I pulled out into the Berrimah back streets, my confidence flaking off my bald head like dandruff, the hot road no longer a path to enlightenment but a giant black belt sander whistling by underneath me, ready to grind my arse into failure if I made another mistake. A few k's later I came back and gave Dan the nod to follow me back in the truck over to the hotel. My rotator cup was really giving me problems—the old vibration rattling down my arms made my shoulder sting on every turn—but this was it. Tomorrow we were due to leave. I had made my decision. Clare and I had already talked over the options. She was behind me, but not too happy about it. I would have to overcome my fear: if I backed out now, it would be months before I could pick it all up again and finish.

We pulled into the hotel car park. Dan parked the truck and tentatively walked over with his camera. I gave him the nod. It was painful but I knew I could keep going; tomorrow was on.

19 STAGE FIVE: UNEASY RIDER

Our final morning in Darwin started with some last-minute shopping. Gav and I went into town to get water, food and gas refills for the portable stove. We wandered into a fishing tackle and camping supply store and came out with two compound crossbows, as you do.

I went back to the hotel to pay the bill and explain to my wife why our bank balance was missing some digits—the perfect time to also explain my purchase of the totally-useless-in-the-suburbs-of-Perth crossbow. As you can imagine, she wasn't impressed with either explanation, but Clare is cool; she was still behind my decision to continue and backed me up all the way. Without her I would have been lost.

The hotel's business development manager came over and introduced herself while I was turning page after page of the hotel bill. 'Mr Carter, how do you do, I'm Nikki Wright. I hope your stay was comfortable.' She looked good; formal, but not too serious. I wasn't sure what was coming—had Lola been hurling plasma TVs into the pool and setting off all the fire alarms?

What came next was completely unexpected. 'The hotel would like to extend a discount on the bill. How does half price sound?'

'Sounds wonderful, Nikki,' I said, smiling broadly.

She smiled, and nodded to the reception staff. 'Good luck with the rest of your journey.' She shook my hand, swivelled on her high heels and went back to doing good deeds. Again, the universe had come to my aid—in the nick of time, too.

With our wives and kids lined up out the front waving, we had to say goodbye again. This time was more painful than before. Lola's little face looked slightly confused. 'DADDY,' she yelled out as we pulled away. I couldn't look back; her plaintive cry hurt more than my sore body.

While I was in Darwin, I had done another ABC Radio interview. I had also done several phone interviews roadside along the way. We had been lucky with the media on this trip, and now the interest was really picking up. Random people were starting to recognise the bike. 'Is that the veggie burner?' some would ask. Others had me posing in photos. A lot of people seemed really enthusiastic about what we were doing. 'Wow, is that the bike? Good on ya.' Rather than kebabs in the face, I was getting the thumbs-up from overtaking cars. And the truckies went from something to be feared and avoided to princes of the highway. They got on the radio to talk about the bike; I sat there listening to the chatter. 'Looks like a cunt of a way to get around,' said one. 'Our washing machine's got more grunt,' said another. But now they gave me a heads-up and a wide berth, always with a honk and a nod. On ya, fellas.

We burbled out of Darwin's lush green setting, back down to Katherine and then on to the Victoria Highway, towards our first night's stop in Victoria River. I was now over two weeks behind schedule, two bike rebuilds over budget and too far gone with an increasing obsession with the horizon. Night came but we pushed on. Through my pain I became incredibly focused and ready. I dodged the occasional blown truck tyre and everything else that came out to get me that night: cattle, donkeys, roos, all having a surprise midnight street party. However, I did trade places with the truck and let Gav take the lead: he had the bull bar.

When we finally pulled into Victoria River late that night I was beyond any stuffed I'd ever been. I fell off the bike and into a deep donga sleep, waking up with a start at three in the morning, rising slowly and painfully in need of a toilet. Gav and Dan were still up, running about in the dark with flashlights and freaking out at all the cane toads. There were thousands of them; wherever Dan shone light the ground was hopping. Gav appeared to have some sort of inherent fear of the toad. 'Fuck.' He jumped. 'Oh, shit.' He ran for the porch. 'They're everywhere.' I found that fascinating; here's a guy who will wade into a fistfight in a crowded bar without blinking an eye, but he was running for his life from a toad. But then again, I react the same way to cockroaches and spiders, so I can't talk.

Perhaps it's got something to do with what you were exposed to as a kid. After all, back in Scotland where Gav grew up, the amphibians don't get this big, the wildlife rarely eats you and the road kill is usually a squirrel or a hedgehog, not a bloated, 300-pound blowfly-maggot-infested cow with a 50-pound giant eagle sitting on it giving you its best 'fuck off, it's mine' look.

After having a good laugh at Gav, I stumbled back to bed for three hours. When I woke again at sunrise, I thought I was still dreaming. Overnight the harsh, sun-blasted dusty brown earth had been replaced by lush monsoonal shades of green. The difference was startling, just beautiful. Mother Nature had clearly also pulled in last night for a donga and a sandwich. Cue flocks of NapiSan-white cockatoos flying past. Cue friendly wave from the truck driver next door. Cue the smell of real coffee and an egg-and-bacon roll.

'This place is a welcome sight,' said Gav. He was standing out the front of his donga, bollock-naked with a fag dangling from his bottom lip. The chatty truck driver next door explained why the place was so fertile. 'It's the Wet, mate.'

I had heard people in Darwin talking about 'the Wet'. Apparently, for six months a year up here it rains Noah's Ark kind of rain. 'The new bridge should make a difference,' the truckie said; seemingly, before the bridge was built this place would be cut off from the rest of the world for months due to flooding. Years back, the volume of water hurtling down the Daly River every seven minutes during the monsoon was measured as equal to the entire contents of Sydney Harbour.

The people up here are very hardy and adaptable. I would have thought the Wet must put a terrible strain on everyone, but apparently not. In fact, the general reaction to the Wet was: 'Good, no more tourists for a while—we can have the place to ourselves for a bit.'

We pulled over in Timber Creek, where we had to phone Bullo River Station, our accommodation for the night, and let them know we were on the way. Sounded simple enough, only Gav's work phone rang while we were there, and he was on it for ages. I threw water over him, pleaded with him, abused him, but nothing gets Gav off the phone before he's ready. Finally we set off on the last 100 k's of blacktop we'd see for a while.

Bullo River is one of those places you get to experience only once in a lifetime, a full-on working cattle station planted in some of the most awe-inspiring country on earth. We found the gate just off the highway, and Dan jumped from the truck, camera in hand, to get the obligatory entrance shot, when we heard a horn. A big BMW GS pulled in behind us, and the rider strolled up and introduced himself as Simon. I recognised him straightaway: we'd been passing each other on the road for weeks; or rather, he went past me at light speed, got to where he was going and stayed for a few days. By the time he was ready to leave, I would finally hit town. We'd seen each other at a series of service stations too; the boys would be filling up the truck and he would blat past, waving. Now he had been about to zap past me again, until he saw us pull over so he'd stopped to say hello at last.

He was a nice guy. We stood there in the heat sweating and swapping road tales for a good hour, until it was Gav's turn to start hurrying me up. Simon and I made a plan to meet in Broome for beers and bullshit, and then we set off on the unsealed road to Bullo.

There is no easygoing, laid-back Territory introduction to offroad riding. For a conventional rider the usual deal would be to have plenty of armour and hit the track at speed. If you hit corrugations or deep sand, well, you flogged it, and the bike would plane over the top. I didn't have the sudden burst of power to dial up or unlimited amounts of torque, thanks to Betty's smaller rear sprocket. The CVT belt would start to spin and smoke under too much of an incline.

The 75 k's to Bullo was a mix of everything. It started as corrugations, formed by years of trucks passing over the dirt. These buggers were punctuated by sudden, deep tennis-court-sized holes full of soft bull dust. Hitting them was terrifying because I instantly lost all my torque and speed. Thump! The front wheel would sink; it took all my strength to avoid a flight over the handlebars while the bike snaked wildly left to right. Back to the c-c-c-c-c-c-c-corrugations until I picked up enough speed to get over the top. My shoulder and leg were throbbing. My kidneys and liver were starting to jiggle their way out of my mouth. Another patch of bull dust, and BANG, I went down.

The first fall didn't hurt at all, the second only made me drug-dependent, but the third had me on my knees. It wasn't much to look at; I was only doing about ten kilometres per hour when the front wheel just dug in once again and stopped. I just didn't have the upper body strength to rake back the handlebars; I went over on my side, my cracked ribs recracked, my whole face creased in pain as though I'd got a noseful of wasabi.

Betty's impeller hoovered in bull dust, the whole right side of the handlebar was buried in the ground, her throttle wide open. The engine screamed as she choked down dirt-filled air and spewed out thick white smoke.

Gav rushed over. 'What can I do?' he yelled over the squealing engine. Betty's back wheel was spinning, throwing out oil and dirt. I was too winded to answer, so he bolted to the back of the truck and came back with a pair of pliers to cut the throttle line. I knew the bike couldn't take much more, so I sat up, grabbed the buried handlebar and pushed the heavy machine up. The back wheel bit into the dust. I twisted the throttle back and she stopped. I fell back, my ribs and shoulder burning, spasms of white-hot pain in my lungs.

Gav helped me up and lifted my leg over the bike for me. We had to push on; we were so close. I was sore, but by now I was getting better at blanking it out.

Bullo appeared at dusk through magnificent ghost gums decorated like Christmas trees with thousands of cockatoos preparing to roost. Wallabies and grey kangaroos scattered in their hundreds at our arrival, bounding in every direction. It was an explosion of life, nature and beauty like I've never seen before. I fell off the bike in the front yard of the station house. Ruth, one of the staff, came over to greet us with an esky of cold beer; it tasted like the best beer I'd ever had.

We met Marlee, the owner of this magnificent piece of heaven. Her husband Franz was away at the time. Marlee runs the place; she's one of the most capable people I've ever met—there's nothing she can't do. She sat down to dinner with us that night and went through the list of activities we could try on the property. We didn't know where to start. The sun slowly faded on Bullo that first night, sending wave after wave of deep orange and red across the sky. I wished Clare was there to see this place.

In the morning a full breakfast was waiting, and we met two more staff members, Trevor and Evan. Rollie-smoking, beer-drinking men in their sixties, they were the nicest fellas to explore this place with. Both men had spent a lifetime in the bush, and had incredible stories and fascinating snippets of information, as well as a fantastic sense of humour.

We jumped in Evan's Landcruiser and drove into the bush then into a valley, past wandering buffalo and bubbling billabongs. We pulled up next to a steep red rock face jutting a few hundred feet out of the earth, and climbed up into the cliff via a track only Evan could have found.

'This place is a sacred site for the Aboriginal people who lived here.' Evan walked us into a deep shaded section only a few metres wide where the cliff wall had split open over the centuries. We were stunned: it was an art gallery, stretching some 30 feet or so along the wall all the way to the top. The rock art was beautiful: the artists had used their mouths to blow pigment over their hands and outstretched fingers and made handprints. The paintings nearer the top dated back some 16,000 years; you could clearly see the image of a Tasmanian tiger. As the cliff section slowly split open, the floor had lowered, and the images nearer the base dated back just 300 years. I've visited art galleries and museums all over the world, but there and then, listening to Evan's soft voice talking about this sacred place, I was mesmerised and felt at peace.

On the ground there were several large boulders that didn't match the other rocks—they looked like polished glass. 'That's thousands of years of human skin and sweat polishing the rock,' Evan said. I was looking at this with my city eyes—of course, it was a table, with chairs at one side; there was a perfectly round bowl worn into the rock and next to it lay the mortar. 'That's where the different pigments were made. We've left it exactly as we found it.' Apparently Franz was out in his chopper one day rounding up cattle when completely by chance he looked down into the split cliff and noticed the colours. He landed to investigate and walked straight into this amazing place.

Gavin was quietly climbing around snapping away with Dan's stills camera; later that day, while Dan and I jumped into a billabong for a swim—only after Evan promised I would not get taken by a croc—he was again busy with the camera. That night after dinner he went off again, crawling around under bushes and hanging off trees like a big deranged Scottish primate, snapping away.

At breakfast the next morning he announced that he was going to get his own camera. Gav had discovered a real passion for photography, and Dan showed him how to use different lenses and change effects. For the rest of the leg, all the way to Broome, Gav was one snap-happy Scotsman. I was pleased to see the change in him, as he went from sizing up everyone in the room to taking their photo.

That morning Trevor took us fishing in the Victoria River. Our little tinny slid down a ten-foot mud bank into the brown water. During the Wet, this place would look amazing. Trev was patient with us; he needed to be, as not one of us had been fishing before. He fired up the outboard and we shot off downstream towards a huge mud bar. 'Gotta get the bait,' he said, leaping out of the boat with a net and a bucket, and running at the edge of the mud bar. When he got to the water thousands of tiny fish scrambled to get away, Trev just threw his net in the water and came back with a bucketful. We all had a go, then noticed the tide had gone out so we had to push the boat out into deeper water. My leg and shoulder were starting to hurt by the time we were waist-deep in the brown water.

'Hop in the boat, Paul.' The tone of Trev's voice and the constant knowledge that the river was teeming with big crocs was enough; I was out of that water so fast I was dry when I landed in the boat.

We started to fish. I didn't know how to cast, or hold the reel, or fish while drinking beer, or bait my hook and drink beer, or any of the man skills everyone up there seemed to be born with. For Trev it must have been like fishing with a kindergarten group; he's used to serious professionals who go up there to do Olympic fishing. He was having a good chuckle at the three of us fumbling about. The second my line landed in the water and I got a bite, I would go into this panicky flap like my mother at a Chanel counter in Paris: 'Oh, oh, Trevor, what do I do, what do I do?' He was pissing himself after the first ten minutes. Gav was loving it, Dan was loving it, I could have sat there all day. Every time a line went in a big fish came out.

Trev pointed over to the trees on the bank some 30 yards away. 'See that eagle, fellas?'

'Er, no.'

He picked up a small catfish he'd pulled out of the river earlier and casually tossed it into the water a few feet from the boat. We sat there gobsmacked as Batman launched out of a treetop, flapped his massive wings a few times and banked hard, turning down for an effortless glide across the surface before extending his talons and snatching the fish from under our noses. 'Good fishin, mate,' said Trev. Amazing. I was back in the mesmerised state I had been in the previous day at the rock art. 'That sea eagle has been following us since we got on the river; I've been treating him for years.' Trevor chuckled.

Evan and Trevor ran rings around our pale sweaty city-boy antics. Their mindset is so different from ours; I wanted to spend more time there than we could. You have to travel this far out to meet people like this. I had so much to learn from them; one day I'll go back to Bullo.

The muster was kicking off the next day. It was done by Marlee in a 'bull catcher'—basically a big old four-wheel drive that looks like it just rolled out of Matt Bromley's *Mad Max* workshop—and a man in a chopper. She normally did all her own flying, but her chopper was out of service.

At dinner we asked Marlee if Dan could go up with the pilot to film the muster. Marlee got on the phone to ask him. 'Sorry guys, he said no, too dangerous.'

However, the next day there was a problem and the chopper couldn't make it, so Marlee had to find another pilot. 'Dave Henry's coming,' she said, smiling. 'You guys are very lucky. If there's anyone who'll take Dan up, it's Dave—ask him tomorrow.' Turned out Mr Henry had more flying hours in the R22 than anyone in the world.

The muster started slowly, moving the cattle down a fence line; we were in the bull catcher with Marlee. She made it all appear so easy, while Dave displayed helicopter aerobatics that simply stunned me. I've spent twenty years crew-changing in choppers, but in comparison to Dave's antics, that's like a city bus next to a racing car.

As Dave expertly manoeuvered through the bush targeting the strays, we moved the herd towards the gate. At lunch I asked Dave if Dan could go up with him. 'Sure,' he said. We asked if he would take the quintessential bike-chasing chopper shot of Betty going flat out across the open paddock. 'Sure,' he said. Marlee had told us that if Dave agreed to do some flying for us, the charge for an hour's flying would be $1000. I was just happy he didn't mind.

Dan climbed into the R22 and got the ride of his life, while I raced Betty all over the place as hard as she would go, Dave buzzing past me like a giant mosquito. I was having a great time. Dave was talking to me over the radio the whole time, as calm and relaxed as if he was on the porch at lunch. He knew exactly what we wanted.

Afterwards he strolled back to the house for a cuppa, while I went off to get my cash stash. I offered it to him, but he refused.

'No worries, Paul, it's on the house.'

I couldn't believe it.

'Are you sure, Dave?' I protested.

'Nah, mate, it was fun. Are you doing anything for charity?' he asked me. I told him my intention was to donate the proceeds of the sale of my support truck when the trip was over.

'Well,' said Dave, 'add it to that.'

Bullo River was something I'll never forget, a huge experience for me—an oasis of natural beauty and peace in the middle of Australia, and right when I needed some serious R&R from the bike. When I can I'm going back with my family; it's just one of those places.

20 STAGE SIX: NUMB

Back to the blacktop, another state, another time zone, another stinking hot day. Fifty degrees and I was cooking. I'd lost ten kilos in the last two months. Strangely enough, it didn't make much difference with Betty; I wasn't moving any faster.

We kept going, all day and half the night. We'd stop at roadhouses to eat and drink and get straight back on the road. Cattle met me for wide-eyed close calls, as did every other critter out looking for a late-night game of dodge-bike. Emus were the best. They have the whole continent to run about in, they can go in any direction that pops into their head, but every time they chose to: a) run alongside the loud funny-smelling bike, overtaking it, or b) dash out into the bush, and then double back, rushing out into the road right on top of the bike to ask the hysterical rider, 'Hey mate, is that thing diesel?'

We pulled up at Halls Creek, then Fitzroy Crossing, finally lumbering, malodorous and sore, into Broome. What an amazing, beautiful place; for anyone arriving from the city it's on super slow mode. It has pristine beaches, pearls, a melting pot of Asian, Aboriginal and European cultures. Everyone I met had a smile and time for a chat.

We found Carrie, who would be my support driver for the Perth leg, absorbed in a book outside her room at the motel. Like everyone in the Downey clan, she's small, but, like Matt, she's a real character. Did I mention she's a physical training instructor with the Australian Navy? That means she's fit—got-muscles-in-her-shit fit.

Gav, Dan and I spent the rest of the day doing our washing and I went through my bike ritual, then we had beers. I met up with Simon, my BMW pal, who had been soaking up the Broome thing for over a week, lucky bastard. We jabbered on into the night. The next day Gav was walking up to the entrance of Broome Airport; he was gonna be missed.

I called Erwin before we left. He was very quiet and I knew something was up. 'I'm sorry mate, I have to go offshore.' Bugger, the last leg was looming and I was down a driver.

There was nothing we could do about it then; we had to hit the road. Carrie was organised, and took care of everything. I was really impressed; she is seriously on the ball. We made incredible time, stopping at the Sandfire Roadhouse halfway to Port Hedland off the Great Northern Highway. We took in the view at Eighty Mile Beach. I stopped to change a CVT belt while Dan watched an electrical storm brewing inland. As we got ready to pull off, lightning hit the ground a few k's away and kicked off a bush fire. So Dan broke out the long lens and did some filming while Carrie brewed up some tea.

I was glad for the break; the vibrations were playing havoc with my hands and arms. I was having trouble just holding on to my mug. Carrie suggested we rig up some sort of grip cover. I had a bit of foam in the back of the truck so we tried that, but it didn't really do anything except make the handlebars look like I had a big rubber dildo over each grip.

Next was Port Hedland for an entree, followed by the main course: oily, overcooked Karratha with extra salt please.

Karratha is all about salt production, mining, oil and gas. More trucks passed me on the way into town than on the entire trip so far; it was just never-ending road freight. I phoned an oilfield mate, Nigel, and went out for a few beers with him that night. In the pub I ran into my friend Brad who works for Chevron; Brad noticed I was having trouble holding a beer. 'Come by the warehouse tomorrow,' he said. 'We've got spare rubber and foam, you can rig up some grip covers.' Another guy there, from Schlumberger, said he had some high-density neoprene as well, and would drop it off with Brad in the morning.

The next day we found the warehouse and set to work. I fiddled with different setups for two hours until I had something that worked. My grips were twice as thick now and the vibration was considerably reduced. Again my mates had helped me through.

Back once more to the blacktop, and more flat-chat roadhouse- and donga-hopping to Carnarvon. This time we rode through endless scrub, which made me feel like I was in preparation for the Nullarbor. We had a great stay in Geraldton, the African Reef Beach Resort; I pulled Betty up right in front of the Indian Ocean and dipped my toe in salt water for the first time in nine weeks. Cleansed, weightless relief. I bobbed about in the water till the sun went down; I was super tired but my hands felt better, and the seafood dinner was sensational.

Our run down the coast into Perth saw the landscape change; the countryside was greener, and the closer I got to my home the more I could feel Clare and Lola pulling me on. One by one, the familiar landmarks started to appear. Soon we hit the outskirts, then my suburb, and finally my street.

The front lawn looked good; as he'd promised, Nick had looked after the place for me, I heaved my weight off the bike and opened the front gate and there they were, my girls. Even Ossy had a hint of recognition for me. I held my wife tight; the warmth of her skin and her familiar laugh put me in a wonderful, restful cotton-wool space. Lola held on to me for much longer than usual. That night I watched her sleeping face for a while, my little girl, happy and safe. I had been gone for ten weeks. I was home, and all I wanted to do was stay. But now, as hard as it seemed, I had to do the last leg, ride from Perth back to Adelaide. I fell into bed that night full of home cooking and deep in-your-own-bed slumber. Even my body was feeling better.

At 2 a.m. I woke with a start: 'MMMMMAWWW.'

Carrie stayed in our spare room, eating fruit and doing one-armed push-ups; Dan stayed over at Gav's, hoovering down beer and salty snacks. I got the truck off for another service, and spent two days trying to find a support driver to replace Erwin. Everyone I called was tied up or offshore. Clare stuck her head in the garage while I paced about with my address book and a glass of whisky. 'Call Matt, he'll do it.'

She was right: Matt was up for it. 'Oh good, I need to eat more salad rolls and hot fuckin chips.' He flew in the next day; I dropped Carrie off and picked Matt up. Dan sobered up and came over looking worse than he had on the day we got into Perth. Betty and the truck were both serviced and polished, and for the last time I kissed my girls, climbed on to Betty and reluctantly made my way out of town.

21 STAGE SEVEN: HARDER THAN YOU THINK

Retracing the trip Clare, Lola and I had done as a family ten weeks earlier was harder than you might think. I would ride past some spot where we'd stopped to brew up all those weeks ago and all my emotional triggers would go off. The very Plain Nullarbor was waiting down the road.

Dan was very quiet; I suspected he was rediscovering the horror of being stuck in a truck cab with Matty endlessly taking the piss and spinning yarns. For Dan it must have felt a bit like being stuck in an elevator with someone poking your brain box with a big stick twelve hours a day.

Southern Cross was right where we left it. Matt started to lose it that night at dinner; the buffet displayed several different types of salad, none of which he could eat. I stood next to him with my plate piled high, pointing at each one in turn. 'What about that one?' 'Got cheese in it.' I'd point at another. 'Mayo.' Another. 'Fuckin egg.' The last one. 'Ham, Pauli, dead pig.'

I went back to the table. Dan was starting to look a bit like a junkie: he hadn't shaved for a few weeks, he was pale and his cheeks were drawn. The waitress came over. 'Anything else, gentlemen?' Dan ordered a beer, I asked for a Coke.

'Water,' said Matt. 'And a bowl of your finest dust.' She went blank.

'He means a plain salad, no meat, no egg, no cheese, just lettuce, tomato, cucumber, no dressing and a plain bread roll, no butter.'

'Extra dust though,' said Matty. Poor bugger. 'And a bowl of chips.'

The next morning we had coffee sitting outside a small place on the main street. Dan announced through a blocked nose and runny eyes that he was sick. He ran to the toilet, came back for ten minutes, then ran in again.

Matt had his head in the paper. Since the last leg of the trip, he had redone his hair. It was now jet black with a bright pink strip down one side. This made for the odd interesting double take by locals. I was watching a big man in a sleeveless shirt stare at him from inside the coffee shop while he waited for his morning latte.

A gaggle of early-retirement red Ducati roosters showed up with matching $1000 lids and no wear on their tyres. They strutted about pecking at each other's bikes for a bit, then mooched over to take a morbid but sympathetic curiosity in Betty's plumage. To them it no doubt appeared she was just a nasty twenty-dollar crack whore with a university sticker on her tank. Then they started scanning for the rider. We got pinged on the far table. The head rooster squeaked over in his leather Ducati pants. 'I hope they're paying you to ride that thing.' He pulled out a cigar and manned up, nipping the end off with his teeth. What a tinea of a human.

'Good morning.' I smiled and finished my coffee.

'So.' Rooster One was not giving up. 'Is it part of some experiment?'

I just couldn't be fucked. 'Sort of.'

Dan, who had returned from the toilet looking paler than before, looked at his camera on the table. *He's thinking about picking it up, no, don't touch the camera, Danny, or this punisher will puff up his feathers and start making an even bigger ponce of himself.*

Rooster One fired up his Romeo and tried to think of something to say. 'It looks like it couldn't pull the skin off a rice pudding.' He grinned.

Matty was apparently ignoring all of this, hiding behind the newspaper, but I just knew he was going to say something soon. Dan was looking really bad. After three months of living in each other's pockets I knew him well now. He was sitting there clenching and sweating; too polite to just walk off, he'd rather sit there and shit himself.

Rooster One was still not sure who the rider was; I wasn't in my gear yet and the helmet was sitting under the table.

'You haven't come all the way from Adelaide on that thing have you?' said Rooster One.

He's going to engage . . . oh no, Dan, don't engage—DAN.

'Are they all Ducatis?' Aw fuck.

'Yup,' said Rooster One, visibly preening. 'We're on a run for the day, you know, throw them into a few corners and hammer the adrenalin.'

Dan looked like Rooster One had just pulled out his cock and pissed in his face.

'Is that thing diesel?' Rooster One asked at last.

'Fuck off, mate.' Matt finally let go.

'Excuse me?' Rooster One was clearly not a fighting cock, you could see it in his eyes.

'Leave us alone.' Dan jumped up and Rooster One jumped back, dropping his $100 cigar.

'He's sick.' I smiled. Poor Danny. 'Sorry, we're just tired. Enjoy your ride.'

Rooster One went back to the gaggle. They glared at us for a bit then roared off. The big guy with no sleeves came out with his latte. 'What a fuckwit,' he said. 'Good luck on the chip burner, Paul.'

I love it.

We detoured off the highway to Kalgoorlie for lunch; Dan found a chemist and parked himself outside a coffee shop with a muffin. Matt and I wandered up the main street and back down the other side. Typhoid Danny was not feeling any better, so we kept going. That night we were in Norseman. Dan crashed early, full of Lomotil and flu night meds, and I sat up with Matty watching old horror films. The couple in the room next door had a fight; Matty was about to go over and join in but then they started shagging, though at first I thought he was murdering her. Together Matty and I got drunk and took it in turns to fart on Dan's head. Childish? You betcha.

Then before I knew it, it was 6 a.m., and I was back on the Eyre Highway, about to start Australia's longest, straightest, dullest bit again. Dan staggered into the cab, looking like he'd just spent the last three months living underground. As I rode I was thinking about Lola; I wondered what she was doing—would she be out at playgroup with Clare? I was miles away in the cotton wool, thinking about my girls, when BANG!—a punch in the head. I swerved, looked back; I couldn't believe it, a bird had clocked me. A wind-blown line of blood tracked across my visor. Right, I thought, pay attention; worry less, ride more, and watch out for air traffic.

The road ahead was an agonising hollow motorcycle shaker into scrub emptiness. We stopped so Dan could shoot the big open nothing, and then got on the road again. And so we continued: shoot again, go again.

'Dan's freaking out about the lack of footage.' Matt came over on the radio while Typhoid Danny stumbled into a mud flat with his camera. 'He's panic shooting mud now.' I think Dan was developing Stockholm Syndrome; in his weakened state, Matt had devoured him.

At the halfway mark across the Nullarbor, Madura Pass made for a hilly bit, a nice change, and we spent the night there. I tried to get Dan to eat the quiche.

I'd done all this before with the girls, and it didn't feel much different on the bike. The road was just mind-numbingly boring, an endless unrolling of blacktop, a long line of nothing. Those three days across the Nullarbor were a seamless blur of one long road punctuated by a sick cameraman, a demented driver, and a border crossing. We were burnt out.

On the morning we left Ceduna, it suddenly got cold, and the wind picked up as the day wore on. We just kept going; by nightfall I was a wreck, the road was slippery and I needed to refuel. 'Pulling over, mate.'

Matty swung over to the side of the road and killed the engine. Dan was asleep in the cab and Matt fell asleep at the wheel before I'd finished doing my bio thing. I turned off the fuel pump, stowed the line and zipped shut the flap. The truck's lights caught the rain starting to fall: gently at first, then it bucketed down. I changed the CVT belt, checked the oil, and then I just stood there looking through the truck's windscreen at the guys, both fast asleep. The wind whipped past me, flapping the tarp covering the truck's cage. Water was cascading down the glass, and I knew that inside the boys had the heater on. I was so tired; it was like my internal bike had just gone down through its gearbox from fifth to neutral while I was standing there: *wwwhm, wwwhm, wwwhm, wwwhm*. I pictured myself getting motivated. Harden up, I said to myself. I thought about pushing on to Adelaide, when suddenly there was a rhythmical squeak and a little Japanese guy on a bicycle loaded like a Pakistani mule pulled up beside me.

'Good evening.' He cut a big smile.

'Where did you come from?'

'Sydney.' He beamed. 'On the way to Perth.'

He had to be 50. If he could do it, so could I. Would I give up? Would I fuck. 'Would you like some tea?' I asked.

I like the pub in Kimba, the Community Hotel. We had a feast in there that night. One more day on the road and we'd be done. A few people came up with words of encouragement. Matt looked rested and ate well for once, and Dan was on the mend too, chatting up a blonde at the bar. My phone rang. It was a guy called Jock from the Australian Motorcycle Association; he'd been following the ride online and asked if a few of the members could join up with me in Port Wakefield the next day and ride with me into Adelaide. I was chuffed; I never thought anyone would want to join up and ride with me.

The next morning, riding into a feral head wind, we rounded into Port Augusta and found our rally point. There were eight bikes waiting, a really nice group of men and women. Those last 100 k's were wonderful. I stopped just outside the city and called Colin.

'The press are here, you on time?' He sounded excited.

'I'll be there in twenty minutes mate.'

'See you then.'

The plan was to ride back to exactly the same spot from where I had left three months ago. I left Dan and Matty behind; riding through the last set of lights and into the university grounds felt surreal. I couldn't believe the bike and I had made it. Then I looked around, bewildered: there was no sign of any media. Colin, Rob, Phil, Steve and the mechanical engineering students were all standing on the far side. As we all pulled up, Colin ran over.

'You're never going to believe this.' He rubbed his hand over his face. 'Everyone just bolted down the road on foot, five minutes ago. Apparently the Premier of South Australia just called a press conference to deny shagging a parliamentary waitress in his office.'

I was gobsmacked. 'You're kidding.'

'Sorry mate, bigger story.'

'Let's have a drink.'

I looked over to see a familiar face. It was Rob Egan, my biggest sponsor, all the way from Singapore. He shook my hand. 'Well done, mate.'

It was weird standing there surrounded by people after spending so much time alone with my thoughts on the bike. Now I was getting bombarded with questions and going blank. It was over. I was so familiar with Betty that I just expected to get back on her, ride off and keep going. But it was done. Now, weirdly, I didn't want it to be over. I didn't want to leave Adelaide and leave that bike behind.

Finally, Dan and Matty pulled up. In the morning they were flying back to Sydney. Poor Dan's job wasn't over, though; he had nearly 200 hours of footage to go through and turn into a DVD.

Rob took us all out to dinner in a great Italian place close to the uni. The drinking went on all night. Quaily shouted me a flash hotel suite in the city—what a guy. My plan had been to get back in the truck in the morning and, you guessed it, drive it back to Perth. However, as we all went our separate ways that night Rob handed me a business class ticket back home, and told me Ashley Taylor and Ron Currie—two other sponsors—had chipped in to pay for the truck to be freighted back to Perth. I could have kissed him.

I slept the happy sleep of the righteous and woke feeling energised and newly alive. I walked into the uni workshop that morning and started unloading a mass of spare parts, then wandered about looking for Betty like an anxious parent. She had already been stripped; I found her, in the same spot where I'd first laid eyes on her, now just a frame, surrounded by her parts, her wiring splayed out over the floor in an empty room. She was looking very sad indeed, I felt like what identified me with her had been pulled out before I got a chance to say goodbye. We had a connection; after all, she tried to kill me once.

'Don't worry, mate.' Rob came round the corner. 'She's getting rebuilt again. Nice work on the frame and brakes, by the way.'

'That was Matt Bromley,' I said.

Betty was getting a new engine, a new paint job, a new start. The engine I had used was getting mounted on a stand and sent to the National Motorcycle Museum in Nabiac as an exhibit, the first bio-fuelled engine to power a motorcycle round Australia—nice one.

In the meantime, though, Betty's bigger, badder high-speed sister sat out in the main workshop somewhere, waiting for me. I hoped we would get on better than Betty and I had.

Colin came over while I was talking to Rob. 'You're gonna want to see this.'

The last time I saw the High Performance Diesel Motorcycle it was just an engine on a table. I rounded a corner, anticipation rising, and the first thing I saw was

Dan picking up his camera. He moved aside and there it was: long, low, and very mean. Now it was a weapon.

Colin started going all rocket scientist, talking about gearing, thermal dynamics, piston acceleration. But I was long gone. That bike had me at hello. I climbed on, lay over the beast and grabbed the bars.

'You ready for this?' Colin looked buzzed.

I could feel prickles of adrenalin run through my body. Was I ready? Was I fuck.

The current land speed record for a bio diesel motorcycle is 267 kilometres per hour ... Well, not for long.

EPILOGUE

Betty and I did 14,500 k's around Australia.

We did two complete bike rebuilds, chewed up sixteen CVT belts, 600 litres of bio-fuel, four tyres, and two of everything else.

Twelve thousand dollars went to charity and education in Western and South Australia.

I got my bike trip and something to write about.

I sit here now in comfort; nothing's sore or broken, my seat is not vibrating and I can feel my hands again. I wanted another adventure and I got it, but more importantly I realised that I'm not at all what I thought I was. I look at the footage Dan shot and think, 'Wow, you're actually a complete muppet'—but I hope to improve on that.

I'm not a hard-faced, hard-core, well-financed professional traveller, I'm just a regular bloke trying to do something with his fleeting existence on this earth other than just plod through life paying bills. The road trip—this road trip—was to be as much a journey into the darkest reaches of my soul as it was a turning point in my life. I wanted to know if I could do it, all of it. And I did, but only with the help of family, friends and colleagues.

At 40 I'm constantly looking to exorcise my ghosts of respectability in the pursuit of another journey. But now I realise that can't happen anymore. My girls are the real journey I couldn't see through the dream of dust and bio-diesel. It wasn't until I got my first real look at Australia, not until I was thousands of empty miles away from them, that I understood that at last. I set out on the trip wanting to feel like I used to on a bike miles from anywhere, but I didn't, I couldn't. Everything has changed. The internal road that plays out in Clare and Lola's world is where I'm headed.

Well, as soon as I crack 300 on the salt.

ACKNOWLEDGEMENTS

It's with much pride and heartfelt gratitude that I try to start the thank-yous without writing another book in the process. So before I start saying thanks I'll remind you why it's so important that I do say thanks, especially when you consider the global financial market I was lucky enough to get sponsorship from. If I missed you out, I was on drugs.

My wife Clare for the leave pass, for backing me up, for putting up with my madness. Lola for shoving those dummies up my tail pipe. Peter West and Craig Voight for letting me take the time off and for doing my job while I was gone, especially the part when you let me come back even after realising how little I do. Dr Colin Kestell for his unwavering support and total commitment to helping me get this off the ground;

his brilliant students; the guys in the workshop—Rob, Steve and Phil; and all the team at the University of Adelaide—thank you! My drivers for not running me over, for putting things right; in the right order, 'Drug Free' to 'Free Drugs' Howard Fletcher, Shane Edwards, Phil Downey, Mathew Downey, Gavin Kelly and Carrie Downey: you all did me proud. Dan Stevenson for his support, brilliant camera work and ability to drink and shoot at the same time. My dad Alan for so much help along the way. And the outstanding team at Allen & Unwin, especially Catherine Milne for her patience and advice all the way from San Francisco.

My sponsors, all good people who thought I was mad but backed me anyway:

Rob Egan,
Rig Inspection Services

The whole team at
IKM Testing

John Duncan,
Tubular Leasing
Australia

Ashley Taylor, Pentagon
Freight

Greg Quail,
Quail Television

Greg Cooper,
Jet Lube

Thomas Reinbold,
Bestolife

Ross Luck,
Tasman Oil Tools

Dare Jennings,
Deus Ex Machina

Dr Colin D. Kestell, PhD BSc (Hons) CPEng MIEAust MSAE, University of Adelaide

Thanks to the following firms and individuals for their assistance:

Graeme Barton for a great paint job, Ross Luck for so much advice, Paul Bettles, Donald Millar, Neil Boath, Stephen Digby, Ron Currie, Charlie Morgan, Shaun Southwell, Dare Jennings, Ben Monroe, Matt Bromley, Taka Aoyama, Peter Keegan, Arthur Palmer, Anthony Black, Jordan West, Bob Hicks, Lou Amato, Steve Hudson, Siggi Buba, Paul and Christina Blair, Peter Gerrand, Eleanor Collins, Rick Popik, Senior Constable Ben Lavington, Detective Kent Crane, David Easton, Chris Brinkworth for the Macallan and for being a legend, Stephen Yarwood, Sky Di Pietro, Jane De La Vega, Gail Lodge, Peter Hymus, Peter Dewar, Nigel Michalaney, Leo O'Hagan, John Lloyd, James Ward for the DB9, Haydn Harper, Greg Waters, Doug Howard, Dave Sadler, Nigel Begg, Clayton Jacobson, Claire Balart, Liam Kelly, Tim Walker, Nikki Wright, Brad Neenan, Janine McBride, Mitch Elkins, Sue Hines, Christa Munns. The staff at Longreach Hospital, Mel and Kim the paramedics; Marlee, Evan, Trevor and Ruth at Bullo River Station; Dave Henry the chopper pilot; Simon the BMW guy; Rory Panetta at Gimoto Leathers; brilliant photographers Christos Doudakis and Brendan Beirne; the musical Craig Doherty; and Erwin Herczeg—see you on the salt.

Here's to the riders.